# Community Design

Elements of Modern Environmental Landscape and Signage

written by **Masaru Sato**

GRAPHIC-SHA

I

## はじめに

　まちのイメージづくりやサイン計画について相談を受けたり，情報環境の整備について考える度に，その考え方や方法を的確に示す手頃なテキストの必要を感じていた。

　本書は最近踏査したヨーロッパのまちや日本各地の身近な実例をもとに，今話題になっているまちづくりやイメージづくりの基本的な視点と方法をビジュアルにまとめた手引書である。

　まちにはそれぞれ特徴がある。まちの自然と風物，景観，歴史と文化的な資源など，その魅力を確認し，何のために何をクローズアップするのかを整理して考えれば，まちの個性や，どんなデザインがそのまちにふさわしいかがわかってくる。

　その基本は，目新しいデザインを取り入れることではなく，人々がそのまちに誇りを持ち，そのまちを訪れる人が心から楽しめるようにすることである。

　現代のまちはそれ自体がダイナミックなメディアであり，人々が生き生きと活動する舞台である。こう考えれば，従来の土木・建築等のハードウェアをベースにした発想だけでなく，情報やコミュニケーションを基本にしたソフトウェアからの発想も欠かせないことがわかる。単なるモノづくりでなく，総合的な情報環境づくりといった新しい考え方が必要である。

　まちづくりの一環として，各地の自治体でサインやCIがさかんに計画され，それがまちのイメージづくりに役立ち，従来の画一的なやり方とは違った，すぐれた地域活性化の例が現れてきている。モノと人と情報とをうまく調和させたまちづくりは，人々に喜びをもたらす原動力になるにちがいない。

　また，最近は世界的なエコロジカルな視点での発想が求められており，限られた部分の快適さを追及するだけでなく，広く相互の関係を考えた環境への心配りが求められている。

　現実にはさまざまな条件や困難な課題が横たわっているが，まちを大切に思う気持ちとイメージづくりのための柔軟な発想とがマッチすれば，まちの魅力はますます深まると信じている。そうした意味でこの本が少しでもお役に立つことを願っている。

（九州芸術工科大学助教授　佐藤　優）

*Each time I have been consultd about creating images and sign plans for a town, or when thinking about the equipping of an information environment, I have felt the need for a textbook accurately expressing the thoughts and methods on these topics.*

*This book is a visual manual of the basic viewpoints and methods of how to create towns and images, based on actual examples of towns surveyed in Japan and in Europe.*

*Each town has its own unique characteristics. It is possible to determine which aspect to emphasize by studying the town's natural resources, scenery, history and culture. By confirming these points, it is possible to decide what designs are suitable for the particular town in question.*

*The basis for this is not just to incorporate new designs, but to create a town which the residents may be proud of, one which people may visit and truly enjoy themselves in.*

*The modern town is a dynamic media in itself, a stage on which people lead vigorous lives. If thought of this way, it is necessary to change our way of thinking, and to add "software," based on information and communication, to the conventional "hardware" concept of creating objects through engineering and architecture alone. Rather than simply creating objects, this new idea must concentrate on the overall creation of an information environment.*

*I have been noticing lately superior examples of regional activation, in which towns are partly created by self-governing communities vigorously planning signs and CIs, leading to the overall image of the town. This is a different method from the conventional, standard way of designing a town. Towns in which objects, people, and information are harmonized well will no doubt become the driving force in bringing joy to people.*

*In addition, ideas from a world-scale ecological viewpoint are being sought after, and rather than pursuing limited comfort, we must create an environment in which mutual relationships is taken into consideration.*

*Although in reality there are many conditions and difficult issues that are involved, if there is sincere concern for the town, and this matches the flexible concepts of creating an image, I believe that the town's appeal will be strengthened. I hope that this book will be of use in accomplishing this.*

*(Masaru Sato: Associate Professor,*
*Kyushu Institute of Design)*

# 目　次

コミュニティデザイン　魅力あるまちづくりとイメージ計画

はじめに

| | | |
|---|---|---|
| 第1章 | まちの魅力を掘り起こす | 7 |
| | 1.　自然の景観を活用する | 8 |
| | 2.　まちの歴史と文化 | 14 |
| | 3.　まちと人間のかかわり | 20 |
| 第2章 | 景観づくりの手法 | 25 |
| | 1.　景観を形成する要素 | 26 |
| | 2.　空間の意味 | 35 |
| | 3.　景観計画の考え方 | 46 |
| 第3章 | まちづくりとサイン | 63 |
| | 1.　まちづくりとサイン計画 | 64 |
| | 2.　まちの情報のデザイン化 | 80 |
| | 3.　サインの素材と形 | 98 |
| 第4章 | まちづくりの演出 | 109 |
| | 1.　記号としてのストリートファニチュア | 110 |
| | 2.　人のための街路 | 112 |
| | 3.　まちの快適性 | 127 |
| | 4.　人々の活動のバックアップ | 131 |
| 第5章 | 魅力あるまちのCI | 137 |
| | 1.　まちのCIとは何か | 138 |
| | 2.　CI計画の基本 | 143 |
| | 3.　デザインの展開 | 145 |

# Contents

**Community Design**

Elements of Modern Environmental Landscape and Signage

Foreword

| | | |
|---|---|---|
| Chapter 1 | **Uncovering the Town's Charm** | 7 |
| | 1. Utilizing Scenes from Nature | 8 |
| | 2. Preservation of History and Culture | 14 |
| | 3. Relationship Between Town and People | 20 |
| Chapter 2 | **Techniques of Creating Scenes** | 25 |
| | 1. Elements of Scenes | 26 |
| | 2. Definition of Space | 35 |
| | 3. Scenery Plan : Way of Thinking | 46 |
| Chapter 3 | **City Planning and Signs** | 63 |
| | 1. City Planning and Signs | 64 |
| | 2. Designing Town's Information | 80 |
| | 3. materials and Styles of Signs | 98 |
| Chapter 4 | **Representing City Planning** | 109 |
| | 1. Street Furniture as Symbols | 110 |
| | 2. Street for people | 112 |
| | 3. Adding Comforts to a Town | 127 |
| | 4. Back-up of people's Activities | 131 |
| Chapter 5 | **Attractive Town's CI** | 137 |
| | 1. Definition of a Town's CI | 138 |
| | 2. Basics of CI Plan | 143 |
| | 3. Development of Designs | 145 |

# Community Design
### Elements of Modern Environmental Landscape and Signage

●

By Masaru Sato
Copyright 1992 ©

●

ISBN 4–7661 0680–6 C3070

●

Manufactured in Japan
First Edition January 25 1992
Graphic-sha Publishing Co.,Ltd.
1-9-12, Kudan-kita, Chiyoda-ku
Tokyo 102, Japan

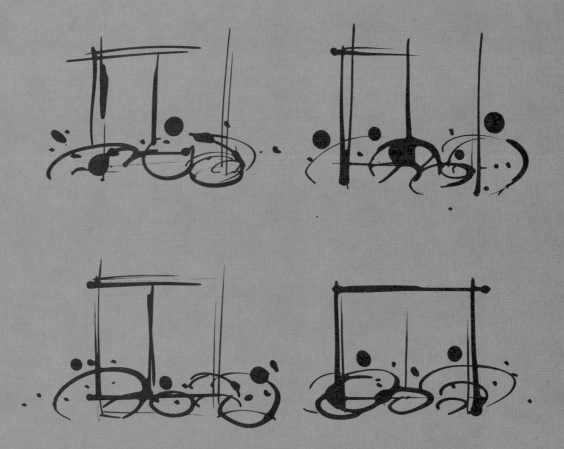

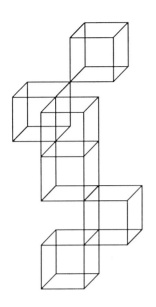

# 1.自然の景観を活用する

Utilizing scenes from Nature

## 自然とは何か

まちづくりの基本方針として取り上げられるコンセプトの一つに「美しい自然に恵まれたまち」がある。日本は島国であり四面を海に囲まれ，山，谷川，平野などがあり，春・夏・秋・冬の四季があって，美しい自然が残されていた。しかし，近年の都市化の波に乗ってそれが失われつつある。

これからのまちづくりは，現在残されている自然との調和を保ち，まちの景観をいかに形づくっていくかにある。都市化がすすんで，エアコンディショニングされた生活になれば，四季の移ろいも窓から眺められた自然の景観も無味乾燥な空間になってしまうおそれがある。

しかも，最近では地球規模の環境悪化の問題が各方面で指摘され，地球の環境がこれ以上悪化しないよう，環境の保全に留意していこうという運動が展開されている。

土地価格が高い日本では都市が高層化していくことは止むを得ないことかもしれないが，だからこそ快適な空間づくりが必要であり，現代のまちづくりでは，自然との調和を目指していかねばならない。それはこれからの21世紀を生きる人たちの，われわれの子孫へのメッセージでもある。自然との調和が取れた空間のデザイン，これが「美しい自然に恵まれた町」というコンセプトへの回答でなければなるまい。こうした自然と人間の関係を見通した視点でのイメージづくりが望ましい。

## The Definition of Nature

One of the concepts often mentioned when discussing the basic concept of creating a town is, "a town blessed with beautiful nature." Japan is an island nation surrounded on all sides by water, having many mountains, streams, and plains. There are four seasons, and beautiful nature once remained in this country. However, with the recent urbanization, this nature is beginning to be lost.

Future cities must be planned by preserving harmony with the nature that is left, considering how to shape the city's scenes. With urbanization comes the spread of air-conditioned lives. We fear that the changes of seasons and scenes of nature viewed from windows will all become part of a cut-and-dried space.

Moreover, the world-wide deterioration of the environment has become an issue in many parts of society, with movements developing to preserve the environment and to stop further deterioration.

Considering the high prices of land in Japan, it may be inevitable that the cities are growing vertically. Because of this phenomenon, however, it is necessary to create a comfortable living space, and it is essential to aim for harmony with nature in today's cities. This is also a message to our descendants, to those who will be living in the 21st century. Designing a space with harmonized nature must be the solution to the concept of "a town blessed with beautiful nature." It is desirable to create images from a viewpoint of the relationship between nature and humans.

アルプスの厳しい山々の懐に抱かれるように存在する家々。そこには厳しい自然と調和する環境への配慮があり，貴重な観光資源になっている。(スイス)

The houses built in the bosom of the severs Alps mountains. We can find consideration to an environment harmonized with the severe nature. The area has becomes an important tourist attraction. (Switzerland)

独特の自然を強調するのではなく，ありふれた光景をそのまま保存しただけでも，その佇まいがまちの特徴となって感動を誘う場面となっている。(ドイツ)まちの美しさは平凡な風景の中にも存在する。イメージづくりへの感性の豊かさが，それを見落とさない。そうした情景を大切にしたい。(佐賀県)

Rather than simply stressing the unique nature, by preserving such a common scene, the atmosphere has become the town's unique characteristic, creating a scene which triggers emotions. (Germany)

山の斜面を切り開いて造成した田畑であるが，天然の石を積み重ねた先人たちの知恵が偲ばれる美しさがある。われわれもこうした英知に学ばねばならない。(福岡県宝珠山村)

These are fields built on the slope of a mountain. There is a beauty reminding us of the wisdom of our ancestors, who piled natural stones on top of each other to create the fields. We need to learn from this wisdom, as well. (Hojusan-mura, Fukuoka Prefecture)

まちの美しさは，平凡な風景の中にも存在する。イメージづくりへの感情の豊かさが，それを見落とさない。そうした情影を大切にしたい。(佐賀県)

A town's beauty may exist within a common scene. The wealth of sensitivity involved in creating an image does not overlook this. We need to take care not to lose such scenery. (Saga Prefecture)

収穫を終えたたんぼで開催される熱気球のイベント。殺風景で広大な初冬の何もない佐賀平野の景観を逆手にとって，ユニークなメッセージを発信するまでに成長した好例。(佐賀市)

A hot air balloon event taking place on paddy fields after the harvest. By using the scene of the early winter, bare, and vast Saga Plains, the event has developed into a good example of a unique message conveyed to the viewers. (Saga City)

## まちの自然

　豊かな自然をまちの財産と考え，その保護や積極的な活用をはかるうえで，もう一度山，川，森，田畑，空など自然の景観を見直して欲しい。自然を有効に活用するにはまち全体の意識の改革が必要である。河川の土手を無機的なコンクリートで固めてしまったり，山の稜線の眺めを鉄塔で隠したり，機能だけを重視した無機的な計画や開発を推しすすめるのではなく，人々が慣れ親しんで来た自然を大切にする配慮が必要であろう。

### Town's Nature

　In the belief that rich nature is the town's asset, and in protecting and actively utilizing nature, we would like you to re-evaluate scenes from nature, such as mountains, rivers, forests, fields, and the sky Although it is necessary to reform the entire town's conscience in order to effectively utilize nature, we should not simply cover the rivers' banks with inorganic concrete, or block the view of mountains with steel towers in order to create an attractive scene. Rather than placing importance solely on function, and promoting such inorganic plans and developments, it is important to take care not to destroy the nature that we have all come to love.

日本では自然が信仰の対象となる。巨石や奇岩もご神体になることが多い。これも自然を畏敬し大切にしてきた心の表れである。(福岡県宝珠山村)

Nature is an object of religion in Japan. Enormous rocks and those of unusual shapes often become objects of worship. This is also an expression of the respect and affection towards nature. (Hojusan-mura, Fukuoka Prefecture)

公園整備の駐車場造成中に出て来た巨大な岩石。石のまち鷹島にふさわしいモニュメントにし，保存されることになった。基本計画をかたくなに実行しようとすれば，破壊するところであるが，行政担当者の知恵によって残されれば，まちのイメージづくりとランドマークとしても役立つ。(長崎県鷹島町)

This huge rock was discovered during the construction of a park's parking lot. It was decided to preserve it as a monument appropriate for Takashima Island, the "Rock City." If the original plan had been followed it would have been destroyed. However, by preserving the rock through the wisdom of the administrator, it became a landmark of the town, and has played a role in the town's image. (Takashima machi, Nagasaki Prefecture)

険しい自然は古来から修業や巡礼などの聖地であった。自然が文化を育んだ好例で，そうした先人たちの知恵に学びたい。(福岡県篠栗町)

This area, with its fierce nature, has historically been a holy place for training and pilgrimages. It is a good example of nature developing a culture. We should learn form such ancestors. (Sasaguri-machi, Fukuoka Prefecture)

川はまちの景観としての財産である。北上川の上流
にあった鉱山からの悪水で汚染された時代もあった
が，賢明な努力によって環境が保全され，今は清流
が蘇るまでになった。(盛岡市)

The river is an asset of the town's scenery.
Although there were times when the river was
contaminated by the water coming from the
mines at the upper stream of the Kitakami River,
the environment has been preserved through
hard work, and clear streams have been brought
back. (Morioka City)

コンクリート護岸。環境破壊と景観形成上の問題点
が指摘されている。川の流れと生態系を考えれば，
デザイン的にも一工夫欲しい。

A concrete shore protector. Issues of the des-
truction of the environment, as well as the structure of scenery are being pointed out. Considering the river's streams and the ecosystem, the
design must be created carefully.

倉敷を流れる川は美観を尊重して早くから整備され
てきた。まちづくりとイメージづくりに一役買って
いる。(岡山県倉敷市)

The river running through Kurashiki has been
equipped from an early date, placing importance on beauty. It plays a role in the creation of
the town and its image. (Kurashiki City,
Okayama Prefecture)

まちを流れる川の汚濁を見直し，本流を暗渠化し，
地上部にせせらぎを設けて親水公園の小道として整
備された。(福岡市黒門通り／撮影：宮本守久)

The corruption of the river running through the
town has been re-evaluated, and the main
stream has been drained, bringing streams to
the ground level. It has been equipped as a path
through the hydrophilic park. (Kuromon-tori,
Fukuoka City / Photo by Morihisa Miyamoto)

## 自然環境との調和

Harmony with the Natural Environment

　自然はそれをそのまま保護することで事足りるというふうに考えられがちであるが，一般に安全で清潔な生活を営むまちづくりには，既存の自然を積極的に活用すると同時に，都市の生活に潤いを与える新しいタイプの人工的な自然の開発も望まれる。どうすれば自然と環境が調和した開発となるか，そのコンセンサスを得るための討議の中から導き出していかねばならない。

Many people seem to believe that it is sufficient to simply preserve nature as it is. However, in order to create a town that provides a safe and clean life-style, the existing nature must be actively utilized. At the same time, it is desirable to add a new type of man-made nature to add comfort to our lives. It is necessary to reach a consensus through debate on how to develop our cities with nature in harmony with the environment.

蔦をはわせた壁，通りにポケットパーク的な憩いの空間を創りだしている。住民がお互いに助け合い，譲りあって生きている情景が想像できる。（ドイツ・モンシャウ）

Walls covered with ivy. A "pocket park" providing repose has been created on the path. We can imagine the residents helping each other in this town. (Germany)

民家の窓を飾る植物。ドイツでは，窓べの花はその家に住む人が生きている証しだとされている。（ドイツ）

Plants decorating the windows of private homes. In Germany the flowers in the windows are said to be proof that the people living there are truly alive. (Germany)

街角を彩る四季の花は，人々に豊かな自然の恵みを感じさせる。ヨーロッパの人たちは，都市空間をお互いに楽しむコンセンサスに満ちている。（ドイツ）

The flowers of the four seasons decorating the street corners convey the blessing of nature to people seeing them. The people of Europe have a mutual enjoyment of city space. (Germany)

緑とのかかわりを重くみて，仮設のイスやテーブル，ペーブメント・デザインにも工夫をこらした通りた通りである。看板もそのまちにふさわしいデザインで，美しい景観となっている。（ドイツ・ツェレ）

Placing importance on the relationship with greenery. the design of the path with temporary chairs. tables. and pavement designs is ingenious. The signs are appropriate for the town, creating a beautiful scene. (Calle, Germany)

苔を主体とし，四季の移り変わりを微妙に楽しむ日本庭園。（京都）

A Japanese garden in which the seasons' changes are subtly enjoyed, with moss as its subject. (Kyoto)

道に面して小さな庭をつくり，道行く人たちに店の存在を心ゆかしく伝えている。（京都）

By making a small garden along the street, the existence of the shop is tastefully conveyed to those walking by. (Kyoto)

日本の壁。古くから伝えられてきた伝統の美が今もなお生きている。時間の経過に磨きがかかり，現代的な造形の解釈からもすぐれたデザインセンスとして評価される。（山口県秋月）

A Japanese wall. The traditional beauty passed down throughout the centuries is still alive. It is viewed as an excellent design from a modern interpretation, as well. (Akizuki, Yamaguchi Prefecture)

展望台の整備によって，まちの景観が一望に見渡せ，このまちがどんなまちであるかがよくわかるようになった。人にはまちの全景をみたいという潜在意識や願望がある。また，まちのイメージを伝えるには非常に有効であり観光資源にもなる。（山口県光市）

The observatory enables people to have a panoramic view of the town. It is now possible to tell what kind of town this is. We all have a subconscious desire to see an entire town. It is also a very effective way of conveying the town's image, and has become a tourist attraction. (Hikari City, Yamaguchi Prefecuture)

ホテルニューオータニの人工屋上庭園。周囲の環境にもマッチしており，宿泊客にくつろぎを与えている。（東京）

The man-made roof garden at the Hotel New Otani. It matches the surrounding environment well, providing comfort to the guests. (Tokyo)

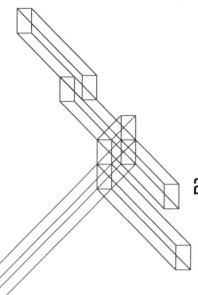

# 2.まちの歴史と文化

Town's History and Culture

中世の自由都市だったまちの誇りを伝えるブレーメンの像。このまちに住む人たちや観光客にもそのまちのイメージと特徴が具体的に伝わってくる。（ドイツ）

Statue of Bremen conveying the pride of this free city of the Middle Ages. The town's image and characteristics are concretely conveyed to the inhabitants and tourists alike. (Germany)

## まちの歴史や文化の記録

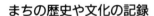

Town's History and Culture's Records

地元の歴史や文化は，あまりにも身近に親しんできたため，見過ごされたり軽視されることが多い。長い歴史をもつ日本は全国いたるところに歴史や文化や伝統が残されている。その歴史や文化や伝統を見直し，再発掘していくのは非常に重要である。いままで研究されてきた古代文化や古代史を塗り替え，歴史の定説を覆す一大発見につながることもある。

歴史や文化は一朝一夕でつくられたものではなく，その地域において人と人とが営々と生を営んで来た結果である。先人たちが残していった足跡でもある。そうした生の営みは伝説などに語り継がれていることもある。こうした記録を後世に伝える試みは人類の知恵の所産でもあった。それらの足跡は神社や仏閣をはじめ地形，山や河川など，工夫次第でいろいろな形として残すことができるであろう。

それは歴史や文化を再認識することにもつながり，また地域への愛着を深め，誇りを生み，今の時代を生きる人たちがお互いに助け合って生きて行かねばならぬ，共同体の構成員としての自覚を促すことにもなる。社会的に古くなったからといって，切り捨ててしまうのではなく，それぞれのまちの小さな歴史と文化の記録が集積されれば，日本全体の大きな歴史と文化の流れを記録することにもなる。そこに新しい歴史と文化がふたたび芽生えるのである。

We become very familiar with our local history and culture, and often overlook them and take them lightly as a result. Because of the long history of this country, there is a great deal of history, culture, and traditions left throughout Japan. It is extremely important to reevaluate Japan's history, culture, and traditions, and to uncover them again. This may lead to repainting the ancient culture and history that have been researched until now, and to major discoveries to overthrow the established theories.

History and culture are not made overnight. They are the result of people assiduously living in that particular district. They are also the footsteps left by our ancestors. Such lives are often passed down through legends. The attempts to pass these records down to later generations were the product of man's wisdom. It is possible to use creativity to preserve these footstops in the shape of shrines, Buddhist temples, as well as landscapes such as mountains and rivers.

This leads to the reconfirmation of history and culture, and deepens the attachment to the area, giving birth to pride. It ultimately promotes the awareness that we are all members of a community, and that we must help each other live in today's society. Rather than eliminating the history or custom because it has become socially outdated, by accumulating each town's small historical and cultural records, we are able to record the flow of the entire nation's history and culture. New histories and cultures will be born from there.

ルツェルンのカペル橋。110枚の絵がまちの歴史を伝えている。このまちを築き上げてきた人たちの努力が伝えられていると同時に，後世の人たちの役割を自覚させる，すぐれた演出である。（スイス）

The Kapllbrücke Bridge in Luern. The 110 pictures covey the city's hisotry. While depicting the efforts of the founders, it is an excellent presentation suggesting to future generations the roles they must play. (Switzerland)

東京・銀座の発祥地であることを示すサイン。まちの歴史がそのサインによって記録されている。（東京・銀座）

A sign indicating that this is the birthplace of Ginza, Tokyo. The town's history is recorded through the sign. (Ginza, Tokyo)

ゲーテが立ち寄ったことを示した民家の壁。形のないものも歴史として残すことによって，そのまちへの愛着を生みまちの魅力となっていく。（ドイツ・ゴスラル）

Wall of a private house showing that Goethe once visited here. Preserving an immaterial fact as history leads to an attachment to the town, and becomes an attraction. (Goslar Germany)

徳川時代に江戸開城について西郷隆盛と勝海舟が会談したことを記録したサイン。こうした記録はまちの歴史教育に役立っている。（東京・港区）

A sign recording the meeting between Takamori Saigo and Kaishu Katsu to discuss the Edo surrender during the Tokugawa Era. Such records assist in educating people of the history of the town. (Minato Ward, Tokyo)

京橋の高欄。橋はなくなったが，昔のものの一部を残し保存することによって，由緒ある場所であったことを人々の記憶に止めることができる。（東京・中央区）

Railing of Kyobashi Bridge. Although the bridge is gone, by preserving part of it, the fact that this is a historical site will remain in the minds of people. (Chuo Ward, Tokyo)

## 歴史と文化の保存

　歴史や文化や伝統は，人々が人工的に創りだしたものである。都市を新しく創りだすことに目を奪われて，まちの昔を顧みることがややもすれば薄れていた。歴史にはそれまで蓄積されてきたまちの重厚さと風格が感じられる。その保存と継承に力をいれるまちが増えているのも事実であり，非常に喜ばしい。どういう形でそれを後世に継承するか，知恵を絞っていただきたい。保存や修復に力を入れることは，まちの有形無形の財産を大事にする意識を高めることにもなるのである。

### Preservation of History and Culture

　History, culture, and traditions are all made by man. We have perhaps been paying too much attention to creating new cities, and have forgotten to look at and learn from our past. The accumulated gravity and character of a town can be seen in history. It is a fact that many towns and cities are placing importance on the preservation and succession of these in recent years. It is necessary to be creative in acceding this information to future generations. Putting effort into the preservation and restoration will lead to a heightened awareness of the importance of the town's material and immaterial assets.

観光地としてのポイントを示すローマのサイン。遠くからもよくわかるが，耐久性に問題がある。(イタリア・ローマ)

A sign in Rome conveying that this is a tourist point. Although it is easy to see from a distance, there is a problem with durability. (Rome, Italy)

昔の城の門につづくイメージを抽象的な造形で表現している。由緒ある場所であったことがわかる。(福岡市)

Images of an old castle gate are expressed in an abstract shape. It is possible to tell that this was once a historial site.

歩道を「歴史の散歩道」として整備し，資料の展示や解説を施した例。住む人にも，ここを訪れる人にも，まちからのメッセージを伝えられる。(福岡市)

An example of equipping a sidewalk as a "Historical Path," displaying and explaining various information and data. Messages are conveyed to those living here, as well as to visitors. (Fukuoka City)

リューベックの船主クラブの建物。現在はレストランになっているが，昔の面影が残っている。こうして保存するのも重要である。(ドイツ)

Building of Lubeck's shipowners' club. Although it is now a restaurant, the former image is maintained. It is important to preserve history in this way. (Germany)

古い家屋の修復と保存は静かなブームとなっている。かなりの費用が掛かるが，まちの歴史を伝えるにはこうした努力は非常に意義がある。（ドイツ）

The restoration and preservation of old homes has become a quiet boom. Although quite costly, such efforts to convey the town's history are very meaningful. (Germany)

まちの身近な歴史や文化をこどもたちに継承することも大切である。（ドイツ）

It is important to convey the local history and culture to children. (Germany)

倉敷市は美観整備地区に力を入れている。明治時代の町並みを保存・記録したもので，その考え方と具体的な表現は，日本各地に大きな影響を与えた。（岡山県倉敷市）

Kurashiki City is putting great effort into the development of aesthetic areas. This example is of the preservation and recording of streets of the Meiji Era. The thoughts and concrete expressions of this project have had great influence on other parts of Japan. (Kurashiki City, Okayama Prefecture)

まちでよく見かけるお地蔵さん。日本の庶民文化を伝えている。お地蔵さんは日常的な願い事を聞き届けてくれる，親しみやすい，地域の守り神でもあった。（福岡県篠栗町）

A Jizo statue often found in Japanese cities. It conveys the mass culture of this country. The Jizo is a friendly, protecting god of the area, listening to the daily prayers of the people. (Sasaguri-machi, Fukuoka Prefecture)

「男の子焼」の窯元。絶えて久しい窯を町の力で復興したもの。まちの文化を創造したすぐれた事業として評価されている。この窯に人気が集まり，まちの活性化に役立っている。（福岡県立花町）

This district is famous for the "Otoko-no-ko" (boy pottery). The kiln, which was not used for years, was restored by the town's people. The industry has been praised for its effort to develop the town's culture. The kiln is gaining popularity, and has given activity to the town.

## まちの芸術

　昔の民具や日常の生活に使っていたものが姿を消しつつある。その一部は高価な芸術品としての評価を得ている。まちが生んだ産業や道具の類いは，昔の人の生活を支えた，地域の環境や立地や環境とも深いかかわりがあった筈である。その地域の特色として，今も根をおろしているものもあれば，生活の変化によって滅びたり失われていったものもある。

　また，同じ使用目的でありながら生活や習慣に支えられ工夫され，その地域独特の形としてまとめあげていったものもある。そのなかには本来の使用目的とはちがって，芸術品として磨かれていったものもある。これらのものは，その地域が生んだ人間の知恵であり，人と地域と歴史が生んだ総合的な知恵の所産でもある。何げない身のまわりのものに焦点を当てることによって，他の地域にはない独特の価値の発見にもつながっていく。それはそのまちの個性化や差別化や特徴づくりにもなり，まちのイメージづくりに役立つものであることを忘れないでいただきたい。それをまた継承して行く努力をすることは非常に大事である。

### Town's Art

　　Old tools and objects used in our ancestors' daily lives are disappearing in recent years. Some of these are now being evaluated as being valuable pieces of art. Industries and tools developed in a certain town must have supported the people's lives, and must have had a deep relationship with the district's environment and location. Some objects still exist, and others have disappeared with the changes in life styles.

　　Some objects have been supported and changed by life styles and traditions, even though the purpose is the same, and have developed into unique objects of the particular region. Some uses have changed from the original purpose, and have developed as objects of art. These are objects of the wisdom of people, and products of a composite wisdom of the people, area, and history. By focusing on common, everyday objects around us, we may discover a unique value in the object. It is important to remember that this leads to determining the unique, distinct, and characteristic qualities of the town, and plays an important role in the creation of the town's image. It is extremely important to accede these to future generations.

南ドイツのアルプスの麓には，壁画の美しい，絵のような町が連なっている。教会の絵画や木彫などを手掛けた職人が多く住んでいた。宗教的な色彩が濃いテーマが多く，まち全体が芸術性の高いまちとなっている。住民と観光客が一体となって共存できる雰囲気がある。まちの奥行きの深さが感じられるとともに，豊かな彩りの中に，優しく清楚なイメージが醸しだされている。学ぶ点が非常に多い。(ドイツ)

There are many picturesque towns with beautiful wall paintings at the foot of southern Germany's Alps mountains. Many artisans responsible for church paintings and wood carvings lived here. The themes are mostly religious, and the entire town is very artistic. The atmosphere enables the residents and tourists to peacefully coexist. While we can comprehend the depth of the town, a kind and pure image is portrayed in the rich coloring. There is a great deal to learn from these examples. (Germany)

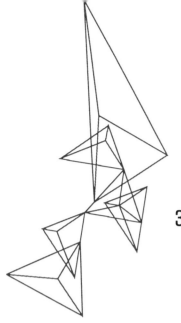

# 3. まちと人間のかかわり

Relationship Between Town and People

## 生活パターンの革新

　誰にとっても一年は365日であり，一日は24時間である。一日，一週間，一カ月，一年という時間の単位の積み重ねによって，人々は生きている。そこには地域に共通したライフスタイルがあり，個人はそれを尊重しながら生きて，地域に独特の習慣を生み出してきた。

　新しいまちづくりに当たっては，そうした習慣のよさに留意しつつ，時代の変化にも適応する，新しい生活の創造があってもよいのではないか。まちは変わらない部分と変化する局面が交錯しながら，21世紀に向かっている。

　既存のライフスタイルが強固であるため，まちのイメージの革新を図ろうとするとき，思いがけない障害となることもある。人間は保守的になることが多く大胆な革新を遂げるには意識の改革が必要であるのは，語るまでもない。

　日本が経済の高度な成長を遂げた時代の結果，まちが都市化し，村・町が市になったり，人口が急増したりした。そうした事情を反映し，古くから住んでいる住民と新しい住民との間に，無用な軋轢を生んだ社会的な問題もある。それが無言の圧力となって，新旧住民の融和を妨げている例もある。

　人の意識の改革がいかに難しいかは，最近ヨーロッパの諸国で変革を強いられている実例や発展途上国の民族問題にも見られる通りである。ここで知恵を絞っていただきたい。

　まちを活性化したい，これは全国の市町村に共通した願いであろう。人間は感情の動物であると同時に，理性の動物でもある。感情と理性をコントロールして行くところにその鍵があると思われる。特に情報の伝達技術が発達した現代では，その地域を閉鎖的に保つことの方が難しく，情報の操作はたやすくない。融和を妨げるマイナスの要因を取り除き，それをプラス要因に変えていくのが，行政に与えられた使命ではないか。融和していくための正しい情報で理性に訴えるとともに，誰にでもわかりやすい情報として感情に訴えていく方法もある。その両方がマッチしたとき，まちのあるべき姿が，別の世界が見えてくるのである。

A year is made up of 365 days, and a day 24 hours. This is the same for everyone. People live by repeating units of time such as days, weeks, months, and years. There is a common lifestyle of the district, and individuals live by respecting this, giving birth to customs unique to the area.

When new town designs are created, we should pay attention to such customs, and create new lifestyles that correspond to the changes in society. Towns are facing the 21st century by crossing unchanging areas and those aspects that are changing.

The strength of the existing lifestyles often interfere with the reformation of the town's image. It is obvious that in order to make bold changes, in an environment in which people are often conservative, we must first reform our way of thinking.

As a result of Japan rapidly developing economically, towns have been urbanized, villages and small towns have become cities, and the populations of these areas have greatly increased. Reflecting such factors, there is the social problem of necessary friction between the original and new residents of a town. There are cases in which this friction has become a silent pressure, preventing the harmony between the two groups.

It is possible to comprehend the difficulty of reforming the way people think by looking at the examples of the recent revolutions in European nations, as well as the racial problems in developing nations. We need to use our wisdom and creativity here.

Wanting to bring activity to a town is the wish of all communities around the country. People are animals of emotion, but at the same time we are also animals of reason. The key is to control both our emotions and reasoning power. In today's society, with a highly developed technology to convey information, it is more difficult to preserve and isolate a district, and the control of information is not easy. It is perhaps the mission of the administrators to remove the negative elements preventing harmony, and to make them positive. While providing accurate information for such harmony, stimulating our reason. It is also necessary to appeal to our emotions by providing information that anyone is able to comprehend. We will be able to see how the ideal "town" appears, and another world, when both are matched.

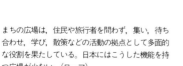

まちの広場は，住民や旅行者を問わず，集い，待ち合わせ，学び，散策などの活動の拠点として多面的な役割を果たしている。日本にはこうした機能を持つ広場が少ない。(ローマ)

Town squares are used by residents and visitors alike for gatherings, meetings, studying, and for taking walks, a place for various types of activities. There are few squares having such functions in Japan. (Rome)

いろいろな人が思い思いにたたずむことができる空間こそ成熟した空間である。（ローマ）

A mature space in which people may pause for their own individual reasons. (Rome)

## 多様な住民の構成

　社会は多くの人で構成されている。都市の形成の問題として，新興住宅があるが，一時期所得や年齢，学歴などを入居の条件とすれば理想のまちが創造されると考えられた時代があったが，あながちそうでもないことがわかってきた。活気のあるまちを構成するには，お年寄りから赤ちゃんまでが混然として暮らす。しかも職業が違い，考え方が違う人がいてこそ社会が成立するという考え方に変わってきた。

　住宅を購入できる所得層が限られたり，新しく移り住んだ人が20年もすれば老齢化して，まち全体が高齢化することなどは，今の日本が抱えている社会的な大きな問題でもある。

　理想かもしれないが，さまざまな職業，世代の人たちが混然一体となって生活を営み，とりわけお年寄りや身体障害者をいたわる心が育つまちにしていきたいものである。

**Composing of Diverse Residents**

　　Society is made up of many people. New housing complexes have become an issue in the problem of the formation of a city. There was a time when it was thought that the ideal town was created by using income, age, and schooling as a condition for moving into one of these new homes. However, we now know that this is not necessarily true. In order to create a lively community, it is necessary for the elderly and newborns to live together in the same community. In addition, it is now believed that a society is formed because people of different occupations and ways of thinking coexist.

　　Serious social issues in today's Japan include the limiting of those who can afford to purchase houses, and the fact that new owners of such homes will be old in 20 years, raising the average age of the town.

　　Although this may be idealistic, we would like to see towns with people of various occupations and generations living together, one in which the elderly and handicapped are especially treated kindly.

空間は人々が活動できることによって価値を生じる。その使われ方を意識しながら設計するのも，広場づくりの要件であろう。

A space gains value by allowing different activities. It is important to consider the usage when designing squares.

## 教育と環境

Education and the Environment

小学生は1年に250日ほど学校に通っている。通学路が決まっていることもあれば，朝来た道とは違った道を帰っていくこともあるだろうが，いずれにしても通いなれた道を年500回辿っている。6年では3000回通う計算になる。ここを黙々と通っているのではなく，挨拶を交わしたり動物や植物を観察したり，あるいはまちの歴史に思いを馳せたりしているだろう。そう考えると，通学路は大きな意味を持ってくる。

大袈裟な教育理論を振りかざすまでもなく，わずかな予算で改良できることから手掛けてみてはどうだろう。都会には都会の，まちやむらにはそれなりの環境があり，学習の材料はいたるところに転がっている。たとえば，田畑で働く意味，理科や社会科などを現実に学ぶチャンスとなったり，地域の生きた生活，歴史，文化などを体験させるなど，アイデアは無限に広がっていく筈である。こうした意味で，教育と環境を捉えれば，まちづくりにサイン性のあるデザインを取り込む意義が明確になっていき，イメージ形成にも役立つのである。

Elementary school students go to school approximately 250 days a year. They may take the same road everyday, or may alter the course in the morning and afternoon. In either case, they take the same, familiar route 500 times a year. This adds up to 3,000 times in six years. Rather than silently walking these streets, they may exchange greetings, observe the animals and plants, or think about the history of their town. When considered this way, the road taken to school is given a greater meaning.

It is not necessary to preach an exaggerated education theory. It is possible to make changes using moderate funds. There are unique environments for cities and smaller towns and villages, and educational materials may be found all over. For example, children may study the reasons for working in fields, or learn about real-life science and social studies. They may personally experience the district's lifestyles, history, and culture. The possibilities are unlimited. In this sense, by capturing education and the environment, the meaning for incorporating designs with symbolism becomes clear, and will play a role in forming the town's images.

府中市の通学路は，デザイナーと市の呼びかけで地域住民，学童の参加で実現した。こどもたちの原画をタイルにするなど，工夫されている。環境デザインに参加させることによって，まちへの愛着が生まれ，教育効果，通学路の楽しさを演出した好例である。

The road leading to a school in Fuchu City was realized through the cooperation of the local residents and school children, urged by the designers and the city. Interesting ideas include using the children's paintings reproduced on tiles. By participating in such designs, people become more attached to their town. This is a successful example showing the educational effect of such projects, as well as the joy of walking to school.

## まちの祭り

祭りは日本の古来からの歴史や伝承に即して行われてきた祭事であるが，最近は四季の風物詩として，またその楽しさの故に観光の目玉になったりして，性格を変えつつある。われわれにも鮮明な記憶が残っているが，神楽太鼓の音を聞いただけでうきうきする衝動に駆られることもある。こどもの頃のこうした思いが祭りを一層振興させている面もある。

祭りには元来の目的であった神仏を祭る，五穀豊饒，大漁，商売繁盛の祈願や感謝のほか，季節の変わり目に開催される行事的色彩の強いものまで，いろいろな形がある。

これをまちづくりのイメージにダブらせて考えれば，祭が潜在的に秘めているエネルギーを活用しない手はないと思う。むしろ，まちの活性化のためにも人びとのエネルギーを結集する形にもとめていくことこそ，まちづくりの一環になるのではないだろうか。

### Town Festivals

Although festivals in Japan have traditionally been adaptations of history and legends, in recent years many have become events celebrating the four seasons, and are now tourist attractions. We have a clear memory of such festivals and often become excited simply by hearing the sound of the festival drums. Such childhood memories help promote the excitement of festivals.

In addition to the original purpose of a festival, to worship gods by praying for and expressing thanks for a large catch or successful business, there are some that are held as celebrations of the changing seasons.

By overlapping images of such festivals with the city planning images, we can utilize the energy subconsciously hidden in festivals. In order to add activity to the community, it is useful to concentrate the people's energy, which will in turn form part of the overall creation of a town.

空間はまちの歴史や文化や習慣と密接に関係している。ヨーロッパの広場は住民にとって，活動の中心となっている。（アーヘン）

Spaces are closely related to the town's history, culture, and traditions. European markets are the center of activity to Europeans. (Aachen)

祭りは大切な地域コミュニケーションの場である。誰もが参加しやすいように工夫する必要がある。

Festivals are important in promoting communication within communities. It is necessary to plan them so that anyone can participate.

祭りを通して老若男女の心からの喜びを創造できる。

Heart-felt joy is born within men and women of all ages through festivals.

## 市（いち）と商業

Markets and Businesses

　門前市をなす，というように「市」は人が多く集まる所であり，原始社会や古代社会では神聖な場所でもあった。そこでは物品の交換が行われ，会合が催された。いまではヨーロッパの中世からあるように，教会や市庁舎の前の広場で開催される「市」の歴史が物語るように，「市」の歴史は，所を変え，品を変え，目的を変えながら連綿とつづいている。

　「市」はまちづくりの一つとしても非常に有効で，アメリカのデイビス市のファーマーズ・マーケットはその成功例である。パリの朝市，東京のアメ横なども「市」の形態が都市の空間に定着したものと考えられる。また観光地などの「朝市」には人気があり，観光客と地元の人たちのコミュニケーションが保たれている。

　最近では，世界的な環境問題ともからんで，不用品の交換市や，ガレージセールが行われたり，行政と商業者と生活者が三位一体となって，ごみのリサイクルが「市」のような賑わいを呈している集いもある。まちの祭りと「市」の感覚が複合された形でのまちづくりも，これからの方向ではなかろうか。

Markets are places in which crowds gather, and were believed to be sacred places in primitive and ancient societies. Goods were exchanged, and meetings held. As seen from the Middle Ages in Europe, markets held in the squares in front of churches and city halls have a history of their own, and have continued uninterrupted over the years, altering their location, goods, and purpose.

Markets are very effective in the creation of a town. The Farmers Market in Davis City, U.S.A., is a good example. The early morning market in Paris, and "Ame-Yoko" street of Tokyo are forms of a market becoming fixed within the space of a city. In addition, morning markets held at famous tourist sites are quite popular, maintaining the communication between visitors and local residents.

As a solution to the recent world-wide environmental issues, exchanging used items in markets and garage sales have become popular. Administrations, businesses, and local residents are becoming one to recycle garbage, in a festive atmosphere. Creating towns in a compound form of a town's festival and market may be the direction of the future.

広場で開かれる「市」は中世からの伝統で，さまざまな「市」は市民の楽しみの一つである。（ベルン）

The markets held in the square are a tradition from the Middle Ages, and are looked forward to by the citizens. (Bern)

市は，珍しいものとの出会い，未知の人との出会いを求めるイベントでもあった。社会的な教育の場でもある。

Markets were once events introducing people to exotic goods and unknown people. They also provide a chance for studying society.

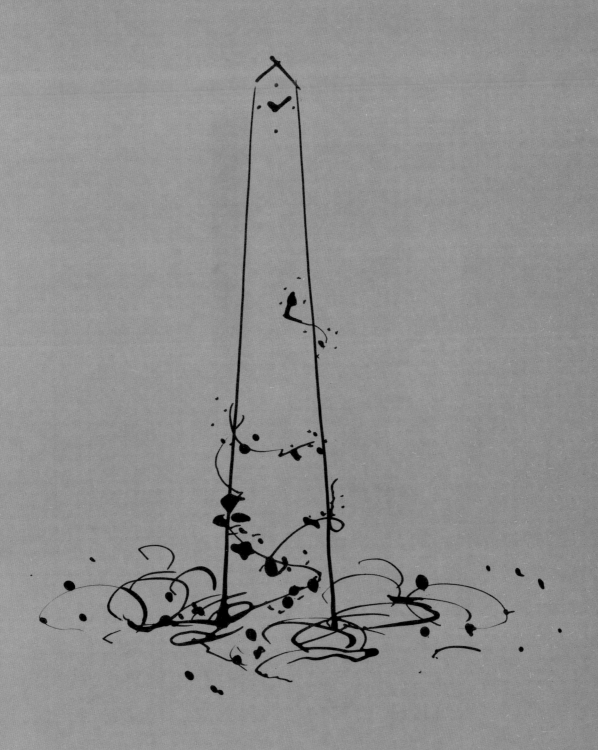

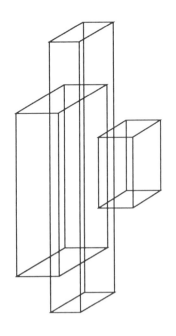

# 1. 景観を形成する要素
### Elements of Scenes

左右と奥の建物，屋外広告，照明，街路の飾り，人，空気…これらの視覚的な要素が複合されて，都市景観の特徴を形成している。

Buildings to the right and left and in the background, outdoor advertisements, lights, decorations of the streets, people, and air. All of these visual elements are combined to form the characteristics of an urban scene.

## 景観とは

　景観とは「見える景色」すべてのことである。景観ということばには受け身でただ漠然とながめる風景や景色と違って，人の意志が加わる人工的なニュアンスがあり，人間が自分の意志で積極的に何かを見ようとしている様子がうかがえる。私たちは，まちをデザインする対象として理解する。そこで「景観」ということばが使われる時には，視覚環境を心地よくコントロールしていこうとする意識を持って見るのである。つまり，まちを美しく見せたい，楽しく見せたい，住みやすい豊かなまちに見せたい，そうした気持ちが含まれている。

　まちを美しく見せるためにはどうしたらよいか，楽しく見せるためにはどうしたらよいか，それが景観を考えるキーワードである。

　そのため，個々の建物をできるだけ芸術的に考えるのも方法の一つであり，ヨーロッパのように屋根の色，窓の形まで規制して全体を統一するのも一つの方法である。日本では京都などの一部を除いて積極的なコントロールをやってこなかったが，最近になってやっと，せめて屋外広告物の規制を強化しようとか，質感の高い町並みづくりをしようといった機運が高まってきた。

　景観づくりの概念には見逃せない大きな特徴がひとつある。それは，個人のわがままな欲求を公共的な価値観のために制限することである。今までは短絡的で個人的な考え方が多く，なかなか全体の利益は理解されなかったが，海外への旅行者が多くなって外国の町並みの素晴らしさを見てきたりして，そのよさを理解できるようになって，まちづくりへの計画的な考え方ができるようになってきた。

## 図と地の関係

　人が描いたものとその背景，または見ているものとその背景との関係を「図＝figure」と「地＝ground」という。ものの見え方には常に図と地の関係があり，景観の中でも単独のものとして見られやすいものとその背景になりやすいものとがある。

　風景は一般に地であり，建物は図である。道路は地でありそこに設置されたサイン類は図である。しかし，常にこの関係が決まっているわけではなく，広大な平野の中を一直線に伸びる一本の道は図になり，美しく舗装された道が建物よりも図的に見えるときもある。つまり，図と地の関係は相対的なものであり，表現の仕方や人の興味のあり方によっても変わるものである。

　一番手前にある大きな木は，後ろにある森よりも図的に見え，森は空より図的に見えるが，森の紅葉や天候に興味を持てば図と地の関係は直ちに逆転する。そこで物が図的で風景が地的だと決めつける既成概念にとらわれず，図と地の関係を考えれば，景観をまた違った角度から眺めることができる。

　建築家やデザイナーはいつも自分がつくる物を目立たせようとし，図的に考えがちだが，それはひとつのエゴイズムであり，人を引き立たせるための建物，風景を見せるための建物があってもいいのではないか。物をつくるのは目的ではなく，物によって何かを獲得する，これが真の目的である。

　まちの景観づくりではこれが特に重要で，一人の建築家の作品が他を圧して知られることより，まち全体のイメージが統一され強化されることの方がもっと重要である。

　まちの中にベンチを設置するとき，デザイナーはいかに座りやすく，美しく，壊れにくく，地域の特色を生かしたデザインをしたいと考えるが，私たちはしばしば，自然の岩や木の切り株や芝生やガードレールを，心地よいベンチ代わりにしたりする。休憩場所が必要だといって直ちにベンチを置くという発想は短絡的すぎる。

　物を図的に考えるだけでなく，環境の特徴や利用者の行動を中心に据えて考えれば，今までの設計方針とは違った発想が生まれていくと思う。また，その反対に，道路や空のように，今まで地的であると思われていたものを図的に見せることによって，新鮮な発見ができるかもしれない。このように景観の中の図と地との関係を，もう一度深く考え直してみることをすすめたい。

## What a Scene Means

　A scene is hereafter referred to every view that can be seen. A scene does not mean a view or a sight that is seen vaguely but has more active meaning with a human will to see something, in other words, it is more artificial with human touch. We regard a community as an object of a design. Therefore, when a word 'scene' is used, we see it as to better control a visual environment. We see it with such thoughts as to show a beautiful and cheerful community, and make it to be a place for spending a comfortable life.

　The keyword to think about scenes is how to show a community beautifully and cheerfully. In order to achieve that, one of the possibilities is to treat each building as an artistic creation as much as possible, and it is another to create a total harmony by precisely deciding the color of roofs and the form of windows as seen in Europe. In Japan there had not been a strict control except in a few places such as Kyoto, and only recently appeared a tendency of establishing a strict rule to restrict outdoor advertisements or creating a community of high quality.

　There is an outstanding element in the concept of scene planning; that is, to limit individual desires before public values. Due to many short-sighted and personal ideas, a total benefit was not easily accepted before but as more Japanese travel abroad and are exposed to a beautiful town in foreign countries, more of them begin to understand its goodness, and a concept of community design is improved with more thorough planning.

## Relation of "Figure" and "Ground"

We call the relation of a picture that a man draws and its background, or things and their background as "figure" and "ground". The relationship of figures and grounds always exists in looking at a view, and there are things that tend to be seen distinctively from others and those that are seen as backgrounds.

Roughly speaking, sights are grounds and buildings are figures. Streets are grounds and the signs placed on them are figures. However, the relationship is not always as fixed as such. Sometimes a street which goes straight through a huge plain can be a figure and a beautifully paved street can also be a figure rather than a building. In other words, the relation of a figure and a ground is a relative one and can be changed according to the displays of design and an interest of an observer.

A large tree at the very front is more like a figure than the woods behind, and the woods is a figure compared to the sky, but with an interest on the red leaves in the woods or on the weather the relationship of figures and grounds instantly changes. If you think the relationship of a figure and a ground free from a fixed idea, then you will be able to look at a scene from another perspective.

It is, in a sense, an egoism of an architect or a designer who attempts to make his/her creation outstand as a figure. On the other hand, we need buildings to back up people or to show a surrounding view. The real objective is not to make things but to obtain something through them.

It is a particularly important element in creating a community scene. It is more important to create an unified image of a community than to make known as a work of an architect to overcome the others.

For example, when a bench is displayed in a community, a designer would think of a design in terms of how the bench could be comfortable to sit on beautiful to see, not easily broken, or to be designed based on the locality, but we often utilize things like a natural rock, a stump, a lawn or a guardrail as a bench. It is too much a haste to think of a bench as the only possibility for a place to relax.

A new idea will be brought up by not treating things only as figures and by considering the characteristics of the environment and behaviors of the users more than anything. On the contrary, it will be also true that a new vision can be acquired by looking at those which are usually treated as grounds such as a street and the sky as figures. Thus, we strongly recommend to think over the relation of a figure and a ground in a scene.

図的なもの。ハイデルベルグのゲート。この都市の個性を強くアピールしている。日本のまちは境界があいまいで地的になっているのが多いが、図的にすることが望ましい。

The gate of Heidelberg looks like a figure, symbolizing this city. since there are few such gates in Japan, the boundaries between cities are not clear. It is best to set clear boundaries by building gates or other similar structures.

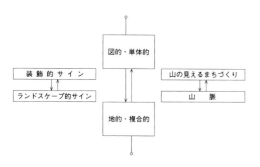

地的なものと図的なものの関係。一般に地面と左右の壁が地的で、旗や奥の教会は図的に見える。

A comparison between objects of the "ground" and "figure." In general, the ground and walls to either side are said to appear as the ground, and the flag and church in the background as a figure.

視覚的な特徴を持つものは他と区別して知覚され、
特別な意味が生じる。富士山は図的に知覚され、象
徴的な意味を持つ。

Objects and places having visual characteristics
are perceived as being different from others, emit-
ting a special meaning. From the sky Mt. Fuji has
the characteristics of a figure, symbolizing
Japan.

地場産業である南部鉄を象徴してデザインしたベン

人の意識によって注目される景観が異なる例。教会、
橋、ドイツの旗、ベンチに座っている人などのいず
れかが、見る人の目的や興味によって図的にクロー
ズアップされてくる。

This is an example showing that the scene being
observed differs depending on the viewer's way
of thinking and awareness. The church, bridge,
German flag, and people sitting on the bench are
perceived as a figure depending on the viewer's
purpose and interests.

ベンチを地化させて環境全体としての個性を創りだ
している例。（福岡市）

This is an example of a bench appearing as the
ground. It matches the surrounding environment, and has unique characteristics. (Fukuoka
City, Fukuoka Prefecture)

地場産業である南部鉄を象徴してデザインしたベン
チ。ベンチを図的に扱ってまちのイメージを演出し
ている。（盛岡市／撮影：武元伸次）

A bench designed to symbolize the local industry
of Nanbu iron. The bench looks like a figure, and
has the role of improving this city's image. (Morioka City/Photographer: Shinji Takemoto)

## 景色の見え方

　景観は，人の視覚と距離との関係によって「近景」「中景」「遠景」の三つに分けられてきた。遠景では全体の雰囲気が伝わり，中景では形の特徴や人の動きなどがわかる。近景になると表情や素材感も感じられる。景観づくりは，その三つの観点が重要である。つまり，全体の調和やまちの統一的なイメージを考えること，視覚的な形の美しさや人の動きなどの機能を考えてみること，快適で心地よい親しみやすい空間にすることなどである。

　これを現代の都市生活で切り離して考えられない交通手段との関係で考えると，「歩行者的な空間」「自動車的な景観」「列車的または飛行機的な景観」に分けられる。歩行者の目には豊かな質感や季節の変化などのディテールを重視する必要があり，自動車の目にはゲートや主要な施設などを認識させる簡潔なインデックスが必要である。列車や飛行機の目には，他のまちとは違う雰囲気を感じさせる，大きな特徴の演出が必要であろう。こうした，まちを見る目をいろんな角度から視点を変えてよく考え，それぞれの場面に対応した情報の表現の仕方や，景観計画を考えねばならない。

### How a Scene Looks

　　　Scenes can be been divided into three groups, near, middle, and distant, according to the relation of a man's visual angle and a distance. In the distant views, an overall atmosphere can be expressed and in the middle views the characteristics of forms and actions of people are expressed. In the near views even the expressions and texture can be perceived. Those three views are important in creating a scene. That is, to pay attention to creating a total harmony and an unified image of a community , to consider the visual beauty of forms and the function of human behavior, or to create a comfortable and friendly space.

　　　In the relation with transportation which can not be ignored in a modern city life, scenes can be divided into those of pedestrians, cars and trains and airplanes. For the eyes of pedestrains details are needed to express quality and seasonal changes, and for the eyes of drivers a compact index is needed to show gates and other major facilities. And for the eyes of trains and airplanes a large-scale presentation which gives characters to the community is preferable. We need to develop an eye to look at communities from various perspectives and to plan a scene or express messages according to each occasion.

遠景，中景，近景を視覚的に巧みに調和させた例。

An example in which the distant, mid-distance, and close-range views are cleverly harmonized.

**遠景**
Distant view

遠景。魅力的な町並みが想像できるが，こまかいディテールは見えない。ここでは町並みに統一感があって美しい。

Distant view. Although we can imagine an attractive town, the details cannot be seen. The town is uniform and beautiful.

**中景**
Mid-distance view

中景。全体の様子がわかり，空間の雰囲気が伝わる。

Mid-distance. The overall state can be understood, and the space's atmosphere is conveyed.

**近景**
Close-range view

近景。素材の表情や細部の形などが観察できる。

Close-range view. The materials and detailed shapes can be observed.

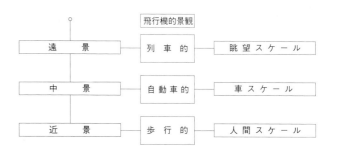

| 遠景 | 列車的 | 眺望スケール |
| 中景 | 自動車的 | 車スケール |
| 近景 | 歩行的 | 人間スケール |

中景。少し歩くところに，魅力的な景観があれば，そこまで行ってみたくなる。そうした期待感を生じるような景観づくりをする。

Mid-distance. If there is an attractive scene nearby, it makes one feel like walking there. Scenes should be created to bring out such feelings of anticipation.

近景。細かく観察できたり触ったりできる景観。物の質感もわかり，印象も強くなる。

Close-range view. Details may be observed and touched. The quality becomes apparent, making a strong impression.

遠景。遠くから見る町並みは，住民にも来訪者にも特別な感情を芽生えさせる。まちで一番美しく見える地点を整備すると効果的である。

Distant view. The town's streets, seen from a distance, trigger special feelings in residents and visitors alike. It is most effective to equip the most beautiful point in a town.

上空からの眺望や景観も重要視されるようになってきた。まち全体の景観計画がますます必要になっている。

Great importance is now being attached to views and scenes observed from the sky. It is even more important now to plan scenes for the entire town.

# アイストップ

Eyestop

都市には人々の視線を引き付けやすい場所がある。行き止まりの道，一段高い場所，視線の流れが止まるところなどである。このようなところには屋外広告物が集中しやすいが，まちの印象を左右する大切な場所として，公共的な配慮が必要である。

まちのなかでは，アイストップによって人々に好印象を与えることができ，その演出いかんによって，訴えたい内容が的確に伝わっていく。こうした点を踏まえてアイストップを計画すればよい。

There are places in cities which draw attention of people such as a dead end of a road and a place one step higher, in other words, places where people's eyes stop. These places tend to be occupied by outdoor advertisements, but a more public consideration is required since they are important spots to decide an image of a community.

It is possible to provide a favorable impression to people by utilizing an eyestop and when it is presented in a right way it can communicate message correctly. Those are the points in planning an eyestop.

ゆるやかにカーブする景観では，アイストップが次々に変化し，人々を飽きさせない。

In gently curving scenes there are many different eye-stoppers, maintaining the attention of viewers.

アイストップが壁になっている景観は圧迫感がある。どこかに息抜きになるものが欲しい。

Scenes in which the eye-stopper is a wall are oppressive. It is necessary to have an object giving the scene a break.

全体の一部分が垣間見え，期待感が次第に大きくなる。

A part of the whole may be glimpsed, gradually increasing one's anticipation.

アイストップを意識した装飾的な壁。人々の目を引き付ける効果がある。

The designer was conscious of an eye-stopper when creating this decorative wall. It has the effect of attracting people's attention.

水平に変化しながら構成される空間。少しづつ見え
てくるインデックスをうまく演出すると，歩くのが
楽しくなる。

A space that changes horizontally. Walking
becomes fun by cleverly portraying the indexes
that gradually become visible.

登っていく空間。目線の位置に踊り場があり，階段
に変化があると疲れにくい。

A climbing space. One becomes less tired when
the landing is placed at eye level and variety is
added to the steps.

左右に視線が動き，その先に行ってみたくなる。　The eye moves from side to side, making the
person want to go further.

アイストップがさまざまに重なり合う変化があると，
行ってみたくなる。

When the eye-stoppers are overlapped and var-
ied one feels like visiting the site.

降りて行く空間。リズム感があり，横に変化がある
と楽しい。

A declining space. It is fun when there is rhythm
and horizontal variety.

## 人と車の視野の違い

　人が地上で見る場合と，車に乗って見る場合では，同じ景観でも見え方が違ってくる。

　歩行者の視野は垂直14度，水平20度で，時速40キロで走っている自動車の運転者の視角は2〜3度という調査結果が出ている。歩行者はほぼ9メートル先の地面を見ており，3階以上の部分はめったに見ない。ドライバーは前を走っているテールランプのあたりを見ていることが多く，視点がとどまる時間も0.2〜0.3秒ときわめて短い。

　その時間に読み取れる文字数は，一般的な地名や漢字とひらがなの混合文字で15文字程度までであった。

　まちのイメージ計画においても，こうした人間の基本的な視覚のメカニズムをよく理解したうえで，目的にあった表現技法を考えていくべきである。

### Difference in Visions of People and Cars

　　The same scene can look differently when seen by a human being standing on the ground and looking from inside a car.

　　Some investigation shows that an eye angle of a pedestrian is 14 degree on a vertical level and 20 degrees on a horizontal level and that of a driver in the car at 40km/h is 2 to 3 degrees. A pedestrian looks at a ground about 9 meters ahead and seldom sees buildings above the third story. A driver often looks at around a tail lamp of the car ahead and the time the eyes stop is short from 0.2 to 0.3 seconds. The number of letters which can be read during that time is about 15 including names of a location in Chinese characters and Japanese alphabets.

　　On planning an image of a community, these basic mechanism of human visions should be fully understood and put into consideration for the proper technique of expression to suite an objective.

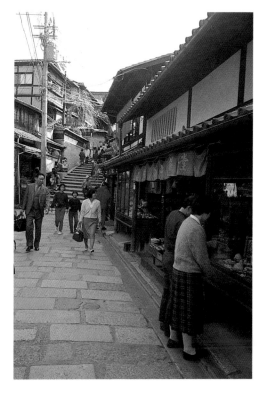

歩行者の視野はおよそ垂直14度水平20度である。したがって歩行者へのサインは，1階から2階部分程度の低い位置に表示する方が効果的である。

The pedestrian's range of vision is approximately 20 degrees vertically and 15 horizontally. For this reason, signs for pedestrians are most effective if displayed at a height between a one- and two-story building.

人の目はいつも動いていて1カ所には0.2〜0.3秒という瞬間しかとどまらない。屋外ではたくさんの情報を一度に伝えようとしても無理で，短い間に興味を抱かせ，好感が得られるようにしなければならない。

The human eye is always moving, staying in one place for no more than 0.2 to 0.3 seconds. It is not possible to convey too much information at once outside. it is necessary to gain the interest of the viewer in a short period of time, giving a favorable impression.

ドライバーの視野は時速40kmの場合，およそ2.3度。ドライバーを対象としたサインは遠くからの視認性がよく，見やすい高さにあって，簡潔な表現にする必要がある。

At a speed of 40km an hour the driver's range of vision is approximately 2.3 degrees. Signs made for drivers must be visible and clear from a distance, at an easily comprehensible height, using concise expressions.

## 夜の景観

　日本でも24時間オープンしている店舗が増えつつある。街路灯が整備され明るくなり，商店の営業時間が長くなり，女性の社会的な進出，各種の文化活動の活性化などによって，都市の24時間化は今後も急速に進展して行くであろう。

　このほか，照明器具の進歩や発達と照明技術の向上によって，夜の景観は昼間の景観とはまた一味違った趣を持っている。照明を上手に使いこなせば，まちの見え方と見せ方が変わってくる。しかも，ある程度まちのイメージを意識的にコントロールできる世界であるから，イメージ計画の段階で照明を上手に使うと効果的である。

#### Night Scenes

　Stores which open 24 hours a day are increasing in Japan. The tendency that cities function 24 hours will even pace up, considering the facts that street lights are improved, stores open longer hours, more women join in the society and various cultural activities flourish.

　Besides, night scenes have a different atmosphere from that in the daytime, due to the improvements of lighting equipments and technology. By utilizing the lights, a community can look different. Therefore, it will be very effective to make use of lights well in the stage of planning an image, for it can control an image of a community intentionally to a certain extent.

クリスマスのライトアップ。都市の季節感や躍動感を演出する。流行のひとつになった。

Christmas lights. These convey the city's seasonality and mood of excitement, and became a fad.

日本の神社の明かり。伝統的な提灯の明かりには日本独特の風情がある。

Lights in a Japanese shrine. There is a unique Japanese air to the traditional lantern's light.

夕方は明かりの色彩が鮮やかに浮き上がり，店舗の明かりもポジティブに見えてくる。彩度の高い色をアクセントに使うと効果的である。

The colors of lights become bright in the evening, and lights in a shop become positive. It is effective to use bright, colorful shades as accents.

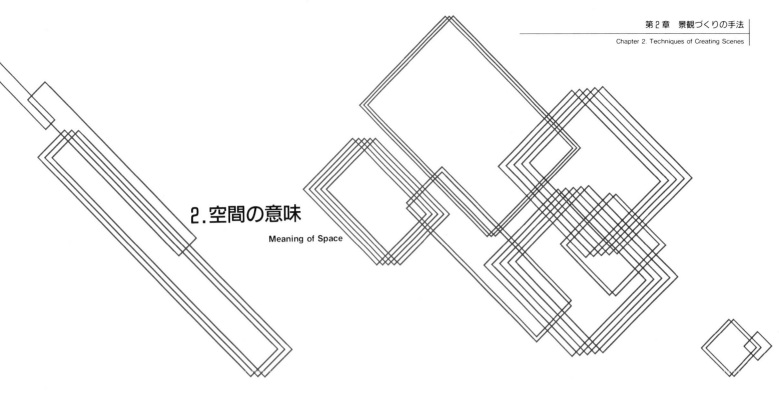

# 2.空間の意味

Meaning of Space

Classification of Space

景観にデザインを加えてまちづくりやイメージづくりをする場合，その場面がどのような空間であるかを理解しておきたい。今までは都市計画法や建築基準法が定める，第1種住居専用地域とか商工業地区とか風致地区とかの分類がなされてきたが，こうした空間の分け方は景観コントロールのための分類にはなじまないので，筆者は空間をつぎのように分類してみた。

1）私的空間

私的空間とは，個人が所有し管理している空間で，個人や家族が肉体的にも精神的にも安息が得られる場所である。プライバシーが守られる快適な場所でなければならない。

2）共有空間

共同で所有し管理しているフレキシブルな空間である。もちろん個人の生活空間の延長として，またコミュニケーションを深める空間として考えておかねばならない。日本では，縁側や路地裏がその役割を果たした時代もあったが，プライバシーを守ることに比重がかけられている今日では，そうした場所がわずらわしいと感じられ，次第に少なくなっている。コミュニケーションの視点では，プライバシーと近隣のコミュニケーションとを同時に保てる共有空間のあり方が問われている。

3）公共空間

市町村，県，国が所有し管理している空間のうち，不特定多数の人に利用される空間である。その他 JR など公益性の高いスペース，ビルやショッピングセンター，劇場，デパートなどさまざまな建築構造物の空間も公共的な空間であり，最近では建物を後退させて敷地の一部を公開空地として一般に公開するようになった。

わが国ではこの公共という概念があいまいで，人々が公に利用できる空間の確保と，快適に利用できる公共空間のデザイン上の検討が大きな課題となっている。

It is necessary to understand what kind of space it is in making a community plan or an image plan. Until now it has been classified commonly as Group 1 Residential Area, Commerce and Industrial Area, Nature Preservation Area and so on by the regulations of the City Planning Law and the Architectual Standard Code. However, such a classification of space does not suite a scene control, so the author attempts to classify space as below.

1) Private Space

Private space is a place owned and managed by an individual and where an individual or a family can rest both mentally and physically. It has to be a comfortable place where privacy can be secured.

2) Common Space

Common space is a flexible space owned and managed collectively. It is of course an extention of a personal living space and also a space to develop communication. In Japan a side porch and an alleyway used to function that way, but in a modern life style which stresses private space such places have begun to disappear. To encourage an active communication, a collective place where both privacy and communication with neighbors are affordable should be further explored.

3) Public Space

Public space is a place owned and managed by public sectors and used commonly. The various architectual structures of high publicness such as JR, shopping centers, theaters and department stores are the examples of the public space, and recently a site for a building has been retreating and a part of it is shown to the public as an open space.

The notion of "public" is very vague in Japan, therefore, reconsideration in obtaining and designing public space which can be used commonly and comfortably is required.

私的空間：公共道路と接する集合住宅の玄関。花が私的空間との区切りを示し狭苦しさを和らげている。住む人の心優しさが感じられる。

Private space: Entrance to a collective housing complex bordering a public road. Flowers act as a border between the road and private space. The residents' compassion can be felt.

## 空間の機能

　今までの空間に対する考え方は，地域を商業地域，工業地域，住居地域などの用途に分けて，地域の発展状況に応じた，主に建築可能な面積や容積率をコントロールするものであった。これからのまちづくりにおいては，空間の持つ機能や意味をコントロールしようとする考え方でなければ，時代の変化に対応できない。

　一方，屋外広告物では，繁華街の中の一般的な考え方や，美観風致地区の規制など，おおまかな指示がなされているに過ぎない。それも全体の景観を考えた上ではなく，安全面への配慮を求めているに過ぎない。

　そうした状況のなかで，京都市では市内を4種類の地域に分類して積極的な景観づくりに意欲を示している。また，横浜市の伊勢佐木町や馬車道の商店街は全体的な協定を結んでまちづくりもするなど，民間レベルでのコンセンサスを得るに至っている。良好な景観づくりのひとつの回答である。

　福岡市のシーサイドももち地区では，全体の地域の特徴を商業エリア，戸建住宅エリアなど8種類に分類して景観のコントロールを行なうことになった。これによってきめ細かい具体的な基準を設け，それぞれが望ましい発展をはかろうというものである。

　今後はこのような景観コントロールの方針を明確にし，地域の特徴を考慮した積極的な計画の立案が望まれる。そのための基本となる地域の機能は次の通りである。

Function of Space

The traditional concept of space is to divide sites into commercial, industrial, and residential areas and control an area and volume constructable according to the conditions of development of the region. In the future community planning, a new concept of controlling the function and meanings of the space can only satisfy the changing demands of the time.

On the other hand, in terms of outdoor advertisements, there are only unstrict directions to regulate designated regions of scenic beauty and common thoughts regarding downtown. Besides, those regulations are not based on an idea of creating a total scene but simply require considerations to the security.

Kyoto City has divided the city into 4 sections and is committed to an active community planning. And commercial districts of Isezaki and Bashamichi in Yokohama City have successfully gained public consensus by establishing a comprehensive agreement for community planning. Those are some of the good examples of scene creations.

In Seaside Momochi Region, Fukuoka City, the total site was divided into 8 areas such as commercial area and residential area as a part of controlling a scene and concrete regulations have been established for each area.

It is necessary to clarify the principles of scene control in the future plans based on the regional characteristics. In order to do so, the fundamental functions of regions are shown in the following.

共有空間：ローマの旧市街の露地裏。窓から会話ができるくらいの近さで，生活を楽しんでいる。

Common space: Back streets of Rome's old city. Life is enjoyed in a closeness enabling conversation between windows of neighboring houses.

共有空間：親の目が届く範囲の安全な遊び場。近隣のコミュニケーションの場としてもすぐれた空間になっている。

Common space: This is a safe play area close enough to the parents to allow them to look over their children. It is also an excellent space for neighborhood communication.

共有空間：工夫された近隣児童公園。全体に思いやりと気配りが感じられ，魅力的な生活空間となっている。

Common space: A creative neighborhood children's park. Consideration can be seen in the overall details, creating an attractive living space.

共有空間：重要な共有空間としての近隣児童公園。ベンチ，砂場，ごみ箱など画一的なのが気になる。10年後20年後に陳腐な公園にならぬよう個性的なデザインの工夫が欲しい。

Common space: A neighborhood children's park acting as an important common space. We notice the standardized designs of the benches, sand box, and trash cans. Unique and creative designs are needed so that the park will not become common-place in 10 or 20 years.

共有空間と公共空間の接点：歩行者を優先させる住宅内の生活道路（撮影：定村俊満）

Contact point between common space and public space: Roads within a housing space giving priority to pedestrians. (Photographer: Toshimitsu Sadamura)

公共空間からの景観：私的な生活が生に露出されると公共的な景観を損ねる。

View from public space: The public scene is harmed when private lives are exposed too realistically.

公共空間への配慮：洗濯物と花では，街路の見た目のよさがまるで違う。花は公共空間を美しく見せる。

Care for public space: The appearance of the street varies drastically depending on whether the wash or flowers are seen. Flowers make the public space appear beautiful.

公共空間としての公園：不特定多数の人が思い思いに利用している。汎用性の高い空間。（ミュンヘン）

Park as public space: Many and unspecified people use the park for different reasons. The space is used for many purposes. (Munich)

## 1）居住空間

都会の都心部では利便性が重視され，合理的な都市生活に期待する面が大きい。郊外の住宅地では，自然とのふれあいや解放感に期待する向きがある。住宅の形態は一戸建，タウンハウス，中層，高層の集合住宅，注文，分譲，賃貸などに分類できるが，まちづくりを進めるうえでは，それぞれの住宅に居住している人の間に価値観の違いがあり，環境の整備にもそれに対応する手法が必要であろう。

### 1) Residential area

Convenience is treated as the most important factor in urban sections in large cities, and the rational life style is best expected. On the other hand, in the residential district of suburbs an exposure to the nature and relaxation are most desired. The forms of residence can be divided into such as a house, townhouse, middle and high class collective house, order made, lots, rental and so on, and in planning a community considerations to the differences of those who live in a respective house as well as to the improvement of the environment are required.

居住空間：古い日本の住宅の例。地域に根を下ろした豊かさと風格が感じとられる。

Living space: An example of an old Japanese house. The wealth and character developed over the years is conveyed.

居住空間：フッガーライの貧民救済のための集合住宅。普通の住宅よりリッチなイメージがある。(ドイツ)

Living space: Collective housing complex built to save the poor of Fuggerei. The image is wealthier than normal housing complexes. (Germany)

居住空間：オープンな区画。近隣とのおおらかな関係が保たれていると想像できる。

Living space: An open section. We can imagine that a magnanimous relationship is maintained with the neighbors.

居住空間：都市部の集合住宅。利便性と合理性が重視され，アクティブに都市生活を楽しむ人たちに似合っている。

Living space: An urban collective housing complex. Convenience and rationality have been emphasized, suiting the people enjoy- ing an active, urban life-style.

## ２）公園空間

　公園には，休憩，運動，学習など多目的な機能がある。自然をそのまま残した公園もあれば，遊戯施設に重点をおいたレジャーランド的なものまで，さまざまである。まち全体を公園と考えてデザインが進められる例もあり，兵庫県などは全県が緑深い公園であるという考えで整備されている。公園は文化のバロメーターといわれるくらい重要なポジションであり，公園を文化として位置付けて整備していくことを期待したい。

### 2) Amusement area

　　　Amusement areas owe various functions such as relaxation, exercises and studies. There are parks which preserve the nature and others are more leisure oriented centering on amusement facilities. There is an example in which a park is designed with an idea that the whole city is a park such as in Hyogo Prefecture where the whole prefecture is considered as a greenery park. Parks are said to be the barometer of culture and are expected to be treated as part of the culture.

公園空間：身近な河川を整備してつくった小さな公園。犬の散歩，ジョギングなどが楽しめる様子がうかがえる。（光市）

Park space: A small park made by equipping a nearby river. We can observe a dog being taken on a walk, and people enjoying jogging. (Hikari City)

公園空間：京都の哲学の道。観光の名所になっている。ネーミングも覚えやすく京都らしい風格がある。（京都）

Park space: Kyoto's Path of Philosophy. This is a popular tourist site. The name is easy to remember, and the atmosphere is typical of Kyoto. (kyoto)

公園空間：昔の王侯貴族の庭園が市民に開放された公園。都市の中の貴重な自然であり，まちのアクセントになっている。（ロンドン）

Park space: An old royal garden that has been opened to the public. It is an important area of nature within the city, acting as an accent. (London)

公園空間：施設型の公園。フライブルクの童話公園。個性的な公園で遠くから人が集まってくる。（ドイツ）

Park space: A facility-style park. It is a Freiburg fairy tale park. Many people visit this unique park from far away. (Germany)

## 3）商業空間

商業空間には，小規模の生活関連商品（コモディティ）を中心とする生活型の商店街や，商業集積とファッショナブルな商品や情報の集積を商品とする地域中核型のショッピングセンターなどがある。また最近では，モータリゼーションを反映した幹線道路にあるロードサイド型店舗が都市の郊外に現われている。一方では，兵庫県の「つかしん」や滋賀県の「楽市楽座」のような一つの「まち」を形成する大型の開発が行われたりしている。

また，大店舗法の規制緩和が行われようとしており，これからの商業空間は大きく変革されていくと予想される。こうした実情をふまえながら，小規模は小規模なりに，大規模は大規模なりに特色をもちながら共存し，地域の人たちにどのような利便性があるか，地域の人にどのように支持されるか，その生き残りと発展の可能性について十分考えたうえで，総合的な商業集積を進めなければならなくなっている。

3) Commercial area

The examples of commercial areas are small-scale commercial streets selling daily commodities and shopping centers based on the whole district for the accumulation of commerce and the sales of fashionable goods and the accumulation of information. Recently a shop on major streets in the suburb of a city has appeared.

On the other hand, the examples of Tsukashin in Hyogo and Rakuichi-Rakuza in Shige show another style of a large-scale community development.

The commercial area will be greatly changed according to the possible relaxation of regulations for the large-scale stores. Therefore, both small-scale and large-scale stores need to co-exist with their respective characters and to pursue the comprehensive accumulation of commerce by considering the convenience for the local people and how to obtain support from them.

商業空間：町並みを整えると全体に魅力が出て，集客力が高まる。個人の利益追求だけに走らず，まち全体が力を合わせて景観づくりをするのが，非常に大事だ。（ドイツ・ツェレ）

Commercial space: The streets become more attractive when they are organized, attracting a greater number of people. Rather than simply seeking individual wealth, it is important for everyone in the town to cooperate in creating attractive scenery. (Celle, Germany)

商業空間：京都三年坂。古都京都の佇まいのよさを感じる。小さな一角ではあるが，みち全体のイメージに大きな影響を与えている。

Commercial space: Sannen-zaka Hill of Kyoto. We have the impression of a wealthy atmosphere of this old city. Although a small corner of the street, this hill has great effect on the overall image.

商業空間の原型：エネルギッシュなディスプレイにも人間味があり，魅力的である。（沖縄）

Prototype of commercial space: A human touch is given to this energetic display, making it very attractive. (Okinawa)

商業空間：浅草仲見世。参道の両側が商業空間として発達した日本の古典的な形態である。（撮影：宮本守久）

Commercial space: Asakusa-Nakamise, Tokyo. This is the traditional style of both sides of the street leading to the temple being developed as a commercial space. (Photographer: Morihisa Miyamoto)

商業空間：パリ，デ・アールの新しいショッピングセンター。地域再開発の好例として世界の注目を集めている。（フランス）

Commercial space: A new shopping center in Forum des Halles, Paris. It is attracting world-wide attention as an example of a successful redevelopment plan. (France)

## 4）交通空間

交通手段は都市を形成する上で重要な要素となっていることは言うまでもない。いろんな交通手段があれば都市は活性化していく。しかし大都市における駐車場の確保の問題もあって，バスや鉄道と自動車との交通をどのように整理していくかが大きな課題になっている。

こうした視点でまちづくりと交通関連の空間をどのように調整していくか，特にモータリゼーション時代のマイカーの普及と公共交通機関との関係を，もう一度見直す必要があり，まちのイメージづくりの上からもその空間をどのようにデザインするかが問題である。

## 4) Transportation area

Transportation is undoubtedly an important factor in city-plannings. With various means of transportation a city becamed active. However, securing parking areas remains as a major problem in the cities and the coordination of the transportation by car and that by bus and train is the main subject to be solved.

It is necessary to arrange spaces related to transportation and community planning from those perspectives, especially to reconsider the relation of public transportation and a car in the time of mortalization.

交通空間：鉄道の駅はまちの拠点であり，顔になる。由布院駅はまちの個性を的確にとらえ新名所になった。（湯布院町）

Transportation space: A railroad station is the base of a city, acting as the city's face, Yufuin Station accurately portrays the city's unique characteristics, and has become a new tourist attraction. (Yufuin-machi)

交通空間：古い港をモダンに改修した福岡市の渡船場。（福岡市）

Transportation space: Fukuoka City's ferry. The old port was reconstructed in a modern design. (Fukuoka City)

交通空間：空港は近代都市の玄関である。パリの空港には個性がある。日本の空港は広告がやたらに目につく。

Transportation space: An airport is the entrance to a modern city. The airport of Pairs is unique. We notice too many advertisements in Japanese airports.

交通空間：由布院駅は待合室を兼ねたギャラリーがあり，芸術の香りがする。

Transportation space: Yufuin Station's waiting lobby is also an art gallery, giving the station an artistic air.

交通空間：仙台駅は歩行者と自動車の道路を2層に分離し，機能と安全に配慮している。（仙台市）

Transportation space: Sendei Station has divided the pedestrian and automobile roads into two levels, paying attention to function and safety. (Sendai City)

交通空間：ヴッパタルの懸垂鉄道。1900年代初頭のダイナミックなデザインで，当時のまちの華やかさが伝わってくる。

Transportation space: Suspended railway of Wuppertal. It is a dynamic design of the early 1900s, conveying the gaiety of the city during those years.

## 5）街路空間

　最近はどの市町村も街路の高品質化に力をいれるようになってきた。街路樹の見直し，照明，ペーブメント，ストリートファニチュア，サインなどを総合的に検討した快適なみちづくりが行われている。これらのすべてを統合して，街路は都市のイメージを形成する大きな役割を持つようになっている。

　街路の整備はまちのイメージ計画にとって非常に有効な手段であり，街路から受ける印象がそのまちの顔になっている。歩きやすいという機能的な面だけではなく，美しいという芸術的かつ個性のある「みち」にしたいものである。

## 5) Street space

　　Every town has started to emphasize the qualification of the streets and a comfortable street planning is promoted by devicing street trees, lights, pavement, street furnitures, and signs. Thus, a street has started to play a very important part in creating an image of a city.

　　Arrangement of streets is a very effective method for an image planning of the community, for an impression of the streets almost decides the community. Not only the function that it is comfortable to walk on the street but the beauty and artistic values should be also explored to create a street full of characters.

街路空間：遊具や彫刻を効果的に配置することによって，やすらぎのある空間となっている。

Street space: By effectively positioning leisure equipment and sculptures, this has becomes a relaxed space.

街路空間：用賀のプロムナード。街路に個性を持たせた点で，街路計画のモデルとして全国に大きな影響を及ぼした。（東京・世田谷区）

Street space: Promenade in Yoga, Tokyo. By adding creativity to the streets, this has become a model for other street plans, having great influence on others around the country. (Setagaya Ward, Tokyo)

街路空間：通りがかりに会話が楽しめる感じの通り。（ドイツ・リンブルグ）

Street space: We can imagine friendly conversations taking place along this street. (Limburg, Germany)

街路空間：近隣の人々との一体感を感じさせる。花とベンチは歓迎の意思表示で，心あたたまる情景となっている。

Street space: A feeling of unity with neighboring people can be felt. The flowers and benches are an indication of a feeling of welcome, creating a warm scene.

## 空間とメッセージ

　空間はメッセージを発散している。こうした観点から空間を考え，そこに住む人たち，そこを訪れる人たちに，どのようなイメージを伝えればよいかを考え空間の計画をしなければならない。

１）居住者に対して

　日常の生活に快適さと親しみやすさを与える空間であること。地域への愛着と誇りを感じさせるものであることが必要である。

２）近隣の人たちに対して

　その地域の施設や場所を案内する的確な情報の伝達は，地域の総合的なコミュニティの促進に役立つ。そこに連帯感が生まれていくものであることが望ましい。

### Space and Message

　A space can convey a message. Therefore, on planning a space it is required to consider what kind of an image you would like to convey to the people who visit the site.

1) For the residents

　A space needs to be comfortable and friendly in the daily life and to express the feelings of fondness and pride for the community.

2) For the people in the neighboring areas

　Proper information of guiding the facilities and spots in the community leads to a comprehensive promotion of the area. A sense of unity is also expected to be brought about.

近隣住民：周辺の自然や歴史の解説は，来訪者にも必要であるが，地域住民への教育的な意味もある。

Neighboring residents: An explanation of the local nature and history is important for visitors. It also helps educate the local residents.

居住者：居住者と近隣住民との接点になる空間。使われ方を予測して余裕のある空間にすれば，地域コミュニティの形成に役立つ。

Inhabitants: Space acting as the point of contact between the inhabitants and neighboring residents. The formation of the community will be helped by predicting the usage, allowing room for changes.

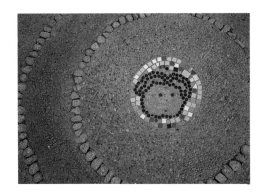

居住者：こどもたちが描いた絵を原画としペーブメントをデザインした。道路に和やかさが出ると同時に，住民の愛着を引き出す効果がある。

Inhabitants: The pavement was designed based on paintings by children. While adding harmony to the street, it has the effect of bringing out a feeling of attachment among the residents.

居住者：団地内駐車場の表示。限られた人たちが使う施設では，この程度の表示で十分である。

Inhabitants: Sign for apartment complex parking lot. When only a limited number of people are using the facility, this scale is sufficient.

## 3）来訪者への配慮

初めて訪れるまちに対して，多くの人は土地に不案内であることによって不安を感じる。どこに何があるか，どういう道をたどれば行き着けるか，そうした面への配慮を加えることによってそのまちの印象は大きく変わって，いいまちだなと実感する。とくに観光開発をする場合，そのまちの特徴を伝える情報の伝達は親切でなければならない。案内の充実は他のまちとの印象の差別化や個性化にもつながる。

## 4）身体障害者への配慮

わが国は身体障害者への配慮が少ないといわれている。ドイツなどで車イスの人々が普通の人と同じように自由に町の中で活動している様子を見ると，その対策の充実ぶりを改めて感じさせられる。ハンディキャップを背負った人たちに対する配慮を十分考えていくべきであり，視・聴覚に障害を持つ人々の意見も取り入れたまちづくりを行うべきであろう。またそれが，具体的なデザインとして開発される技術的な裏づけも必要である。

3) For the visitors

Many of those who visit the town for the first time feel insecure due to the unfamiliarity. By providing information on what kind of spots exist where, which way to take and so on, an impression of the town greatly changes. Especially in touristic developments, the messages to convey the characters of the town have to be in detail. Good guidance can be a key factor for the town to be attractive.

4) For the handicapped

It is said that there is less consideration to the physical handicapped in Japan. Looking at those in the wheel chairs as active as normal people in towns in Germany, for example, one is struck with an idea that substantial work is conducted in such a country. It is necessary to consider those who take care of the handicapped and to listen to the opinions of those with visual and auditory handicaps. At the same time, techniques to back up the concrete design are also needed.

来訪者：遠方からの来訪者も利用する施設は，機能的に表示する。選択肢が多い場合は地図化する。

Visitors: Signs for facilities that are used by visitors from far away must be displayed functionally. If many choices exist, they should be displayed in a map form.

来訪者：小さなホテルの空き部屋表示。親切な情報になっている。

Visitors: Sign indicating vacant rooms at a small hotel. The information is considerate.

身体障害者：視覚に障害のある人たちのための点字ブロック。おおげさなデザインは景観を損ねていると考えるかもしれないが，一般の人々にいたわりの気持ちを抱かせる効果がある。

The handicapped: A braille block for the blind. Although visitors may feel that the exaggerated design harms the view, it has the effect of attracting the sympathy of the general public.

歩行者のための空間は、ゆとりと変化を感じさせる
ものにしたい。水や四季の花で彩る手法が増えてい
る。

Space for pedestrians should offer a sense of
relaxation and variety. Methods using water and
seasonal flowers are becoming popular.

パリではどんなに混雑する道でも、人が歩けるスペ
ースを確保して駐車する。日本のドライバーもこの
マナーに学ぶべきである。

No matter how busy the street is, drivers in Paris
will always park leaving enough space for pedestrians to walk by. Japanese drivers should learn
about manners form this.

バス停は遠くからも見えるようにサインを工夫する。
必要な情報が簡潔に表示されている。

The signs for bus stops should be easily recognizable from a distance. The necessary information
is concisely displayed.

放置された自転車で町の案内サインがふさがれてい
る。全国各地で深刻な社会問題となっている。

An information sign is blocked by abandoned
bicycles. This is becoming a serious social issue
around the country.

乗物を利用しやすくし、施設をきちんと表示するの
は大変重要である。（名古屋市）

It is very important to make vehicles easy to use,
and to clearly indicate the facilities. (Nagoya
City)

美しく飾られた電車。こどもたちに夢と楽しさを与
えている。まちの楽しさや華やかさが演出された好
例。

A beautifully decorated train. It provides fun and
dreams for children. This is a good example of
the gaiety and colorful scenes of the city being
displayed.

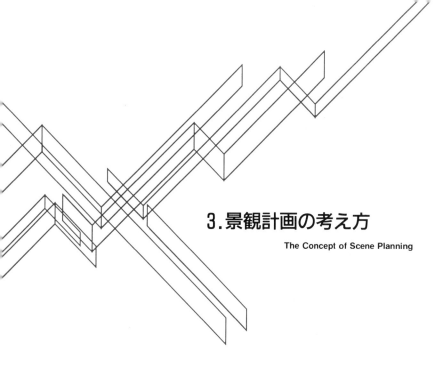

# 3.景観計画の考え方
## The Concept of Scene Planning

## 地域の再生

　現代都市はますます複雑化し高度に成長を遂げつつある。一方では過疎化に悩む現象が各地に現れているが，それらの地域の実情をふまえ，将来のあるべき姿を設定し，まちの活性化を図りたいというのが，各市町村が共通に抱えている問題であろう。都市機能の拡充に対応した空間の効率化と，現代のニーズに合わせたリニューアルが各地で行われている。

　こうした状況のなかで，デザインは大きな一翼を担っている。そのデザインの根本思想の中に捉えておかなければならないのは，機能や効率や経済的という面ばかりではなく，地域の自然や伝統的産業や，その地域ならではの文化の面を十分考慮して，地域を育てていく観点で今後の産業のあり方や商店の商品構成，パッケージなども含めたトータルなデザインを展開するよう心掛けねばならない。

### Redevelopment of Communities

　　　Communities have become more and more complicated and highly developed. Some regions suffer from the depopulation and the local administrations must be committed to the activation of the community by setting a future plan based on the conditions of the area. There are many examples throughout the country to utilize a space more effectively and to renew it by satisfying the present needs according to the expansion of the function of cities.

　　　In such circumstances, design is one of the fields to play an important role. The visions which should be placed at the center of the design are not only these of functions, effectiveness or economy, but an overall design considering nature, traditional industries and cultural aspects.

北九州国際会議場。斬新なデザインで地域活性化の起爆剤になると期待されている。

Northern Kyushu International Conference Hall. Its novel design is expected to trigger activity in the community.

都心部の一角を有効活用する開発計画のコンペが行われた。（福岡市）

A competition was held for ideas on effective uses of a central district. (Fukuoka City)

採用された情報集約ビル「イムズ」。土日には遠方からも人々が集まる。長崎からの特急列車「かもめ号」に因んで「かもめ族」の新語が生まれた。

The adopted design. An intensive data building called Imuz many people travel here from a distance on the weekend. In reference to the express train from Nagasaki, the "Kamome," a now term, the "Kamome Tribe," was created.

新旧の建物が混在し、この数年の動向が注目される。都市にとっては都心部の有効活用が不可避だが、古い情緒のある町並みをどのように残していくかも大きな課題である。

New and old buildings co-exist, and recent movements are gaining attention. Although the effective utilization of city centers are inevitable to the city, how to preserve the old, traditional atmosphere and buildings is also an important topic to consider.

## 建物の個性化

　建築物は地域のイメージに大きな影響を与える。新しいタイプの建物が集積されればなおさらである。問題は，強烈な個性ををを持った建物を奨励するか，ある一定の地域に限って，景観の調和を考えたまち全体としての特徴を出していくかである。無作為に立てられる建物がよいのか，一定の条件を与えて環境との調和を求めるコンセプトにコンセンサスが得られるようにするか，地域の識者の間で討議してもらいたいものである。欧米では古い建物に愛着を持ち大切に保存し，歴史や文化を守って先人たちの遺産を受け継ごうとしている。その姿勢を学ぶべきである。

**Uniqueness of Buildings**

　　　Buildings greatly influence an image of the region. It is more so when new buildings are constructed one after another. The question is either to construct many buildings with strong characters or to consider a total harmony in the scene as a community and create certain characters of the community. Discussion is expected among the intellectuals of the area whether it is good to construct without an concept or to demand a concept or consensus for creating a harmony with the environment that satisfies certain conditions. Not all buildings in Europe are good, but there are much to learn from their attitude to succeed to the historical and cultural properties.

新しいタイプの教会。威圧的なものから，人々に親しみやすいタイプのデザインに変わりつつある。

A new type of church. Designs are changing from those that are overbearing to more approachable ones.

最も美しい教会の一つとされるミラノ大聖堂。都市の象徴として聳えたっている。

The Cathedral of Milano is considered to be one of the most beautiful churches. It has become a symbol of the city.

1889年，パリ博を記念してつくられたエッフェル塔。7400トンの鉄材で高さ296メートルの高さを誇り，まちの象徴が宗教上の教会から技術へと移った。

The Eiffel Tower was built in 1889 to commemorate the Paris Exposition. Using 7400 tons of steel, the tower rises 296 meters into the sky. The city's symbol began to move from religious churches to technology with the construction of this tower.

パリ，ポンピドーセンター。新しい芸術の拠点としての象徴的な意味を持つ。

The Centre National d'Art et de Culture Georges Pompidou in Paris. The center has a symbolic meaning of being the new base of art.

シュバビッシャル（ドイツ）

Schwaäbisch Hall(Germany)

ミラノ

Milano

パリ

Paris

倉敷
まちの景観の中で使われている素材と色がそのまち
のイメージを形作っている。

Kurashiki
The materials and colors used within the city's
scenes form the image of the city.

新しい文化の拠点である東京芸術劇場。池袋界隈の
イメージに大きな影響を及ぼしている。

The Tokyo Art Theater is the new base of culture.
It has had a great influence on the image of Ikebu-
kuro and its surrounding areas.

ロンドン

London

## 景観の形成と材料

　都市の景観を作り上げていく材料は，昔は容易に手にはいりやすい地元産の材料が使われることが多かったが，最近では製造技術の発達と輸送の拡充もあって，多様な材料を広く世界に求める動きがある。

　都市の景観が未来永劫に及ぶのだと考えなくとも，一度作った景観は少なくとも21世紀に受け継がれるものであると自覚すべきである。都市の景観は文化遺産であり，現代のわれわれが次代に贈るメッセージでもある。アスファルトとコンクリートで無造作に固められていた街路を天然石の石畳に変えていくなど，ただ機能的だから良いというのではなく，地域の特徴を生かし年月とともに味わいが深まる素材を使う方向に向かっている。

　それは地域の新しいインフラストラクチャーであると同時に，現代の美意識や価値観を後世に伝えようとする民衆の意志であると評価しておきたい。

### Materials in Scene Planning

　　　The materials for constructing urban communities used to be the local products which are relatively easy to acquire, considering the conditions of the transportation and technical aspects. But recently there is a tendency to explore materials all over the world due to the improvement of production techniques and transportation.

　　　It may be too much to say that urban scenes remain forever, but at least it should be remembered that they are going to be succeeded in the 21st century. They are cultural properties and at the same time are our messages from the present era to the next generation. Examples show a new direction to express locality such as in changing streets made of asphalts and concretes into natural looks and stone pavement.

　　　I would like to evaluate such a tendency as a regional effort to convey modern values, a sense of beauty and state of culture to the later era more than simply as the local infrastructures.

カナダ産の木の歩道。骨太な表情が新鮮である。中央は天の川をイメージし，鋲で星を表している。コンクリートにも豊かな表情をつくれる。

Pedestrian path made of Canadian wood. The strongly built expression is fresh. The center was built in the image of the Milky Way, with tacks expressing stars. It is possible to create a rich expression on concrete, as well.

日本的な石と竹の通路。（京都・高桐院）

A path of stone and bamboo in the Japanese style.(Kotoin, Kyoto)

ミラノの石畳。がっしりと組まれた石の舗装が美しい。巧みな石組みは石の文化の遺産である。

Stone pavement in Milan. The sturdy stone pavement is beautiful. The clever rockwork is inherited from this area's culture of stones.

アーヘン工科大学シュパイデル教授による建築実習。素材は発想やデザインに大きな影響を与える。（漆喰指導：久住）

An architecture training course held at TH. Aachen Pros. Manfred Seidal. The materials have great influence on the images and designs.

地元の産業とのかかわりを考慮したステンレスの四阿。

A stainless steel arbor taking into consideration the local industry.

伝統的な木組みの家並み。木組みの模様には幸福、火除けなどの意味がある。（下図参照）

Houses made of the traditional wooden framework. The patterns of the framework symbolize happiness and protection against fire. (Refer to the photo below)

中世の面影を今に伝えるネルドリンゲンの壁。（ドイツ）

A wall in Novdlingen conveying the image of the Middle Ages. (Germany)

表1）西ドイツ壁面装飾図形の意味

| 図形 | 意味 | 図形 | 意味 |
|---|---|---|---|
| ✕ | 乗法，祝福，財産の増加 | ⚡ | 結婚，おきて |
| ◇ 人 | 人，動物，田畑の肥沃，末永い定住 | ⚡ | 運命の拘束 |
| ✖ | 豊作 | ⌒ ⌒ | 輪，太陽，太陽の運行，防火，光の恵み |
| ✖ ✖ | 財産の増加の願い，豊作 | ○ ☀ | 四季の推移，防火，光の恵み，避雷 |
| ✕ | 神の加護，防火 | ◎ ♀ | 四季の推移，防火，光の恵み，避雷 |
| ✕ | 神の祝福 | 〰 | 落雷よけ |
| ♡ | 女神の象徴，愛のしるし | ☆ ✿ | 不正の防止，いっさいの本質と形 |
| Ⴑ | 子孫繁栄，無病息災 | ✳ | |
| ✻ | 家族の誠実と和 | ꝛ ꒱ | 幸福，健康，祝福 |
| Ψ | 農夫，豊作 | 5 | 勝利，幸福，豊作 |
| / | 誕生，生産の向上 | 人 | 多忙と富 |
| \ | 天寿の全う | ✝ | 輝き，救済，質素な富 |

ドイツの藁ぶき屋根の農家。

A German straw-thatched farm house.

石を外装材として使用した民家。まち全体が地元で産出される石でできていて個性的な景観となっている。（ドイツ・モンシャウ）

Private homes using stones as the exterior material. The entire town is built from local rocks, creating a unique scenery. (Monshau, Germany)

## 環境と色彩

Environment and Colors

「公共の色彩を考える会」は「公共の色彩賞」を毎年選定している。自治体もこれに注目して、都市の中の色彩を真剣に考えはじめているのは非常に頼もしい。

色の選択はその色が持つ心理的な色彩効果とあいまって、環境のイメージを左右する大きな要素である。しかし、古い歴史と伝統のあるまちは、それなりに個性的な色彩をもっており、全体として独特の雰囲気を醸し出している場合が多い。自然環境、気候風土、人情などが複合されて培ってきた色彩であると考えれば、地域の再整備などでそれを一挙に改めてしまうのはどうかと思う。その色彩を選んで醸成してきた連綿とした文化に思いを馳せると、地域特有の色彩はそのまちに生きていた調和のとれた色彩であるとも言えよう。

また、樹木が多いので緑、空や海の青といった、環境に調和させようと類似の色を使うことがあるが、しばしば違和感を感じさせる。景観との調和を考えるならば、安易に類似の色や地味な色を選ぶのは賢明とは言えない。

「穏やか」「活気ある」などのイメージも、色彩の選択によって形成されることが多い。まちの基調色をどう選ぶか、風格のある色彩の選定はどうするかなど、課題も多い。

Environment and Colors

The Committee of Public Colors sponsors the Public Color Award every year. It is good that regional governments pay attention to the award and has started to recognize the importance of colors in the cities.

Selection of colors is an influential factor to decide an image of the environment with their psychological effect. The towns which maintain old history and tradition usually possess unique and particular colors and create a total atmosphere. It may be too hasty to renew those colors that have been created by the surrounding nature, the climate and human history. Considering the culture that has selected and fostered those colors, they are harmoneous colors in the town.

On the contrary, one may sense awkwardness by seeing the colors similar to the environment such as green to match the surrounding trees and blue for the sky and the sea. It is not recommended to use similar colors or conservation colors if the harmony with the scene is considered.

The images such as calm, active and so on are often created by the selection of colors. How to determine the basic tone of the community and how to select a color to create a sense of tradition are only a few examples of the questions in planning a scene. Please refer to the chart of images that colors express.

京都・清水寺の五重の塔の個性的な赤。

The unique red of Kyoto's Kiyomizu-dera Temples five-storied pagoda.

遠野の農家。くすんだ色彩の土壁と浮き出た木組み。大根などをここで乾かす。

Farm house in Tono. The wooden framework shows through the dull colored mud wall. Vegetables such as radishes are dried here.

京都金閣寺への参道の壁。壁と瓦の色に地域の特徴が出されている。

Walls of the approach to Kyoto's Kinkaku-ji Temple. The colors of the walls and tiles represent the district's unique characteristics.

京都御所の壁。

Walls of the Kyoto Imperial Palace.

伏見稲荷の壁。独特の朱色が鮮やかである。

Walls of the Fushimi Inari Shrine. The unique red is very colorful.

倉敷の蔵のイメージを活用したもの。白と黒（グレー）のモノトーンのコントラストが美しい。

The image of a Kurashiki warehouse was utilized. The contrast of white and black (gray) is beautiful.

木組みとシャッターのパターンが美しい。

The patterns of the wooden framework and shutters are beautiful.

城壁を利用した店舗の扉。大胆なパターンと色彩に見事な一体感がある。（ハイデルベルク）

Shop's door using part of a castle wall. The bold patterns and colors have an excellent unity. (Heidelberg)

アクセントになっている色。周囲の環境との調和を考えていかねばならない。

Color acting as an accent. It is necessary to consider the harmony with the surrounding environment.

リンブルグの民家。木の自然な曲がりをそのまま生かした木組みと，鮮やかな色彩で美しく構成されている。（ドイツ）

Private house in Limburg. The wood's natural curves were left unchanged in the framework. Combined with the bright colors used, the overall structure is very beautiful. (Germany)

アーヘンの付属病院。派手な色の鉄骨とガラスで出来ている。

A hospital in Aachen made of brightly colored steel frames and glass.

モンシャウの遠景。鮮やかな赤と黄色の建物が見える。環境の色彩計画では一般に中間色を推奨しがちだが、強い色彩でもアクセントとなって調和する可能性がある。

Distant view of Monshau. Bright red and yellow buildings can be seen. Although neutral colors are often recommended in environmental color schemes, it is possible to harmonize strong colors, as well, since they become accents.

ロンドンのパブ。一面に赤を使ってまとめているが意外にシックな雰囲気になっていた。

A London pub. Although red is used as the main color, the result is unexpectedly chic.

南ドイツのアルプスを背景にした町。黒と黄色が上手に使われ、清潔で温かい、軽やかな印象を与えている。赤や緑の点も映え、信号機の色彩も周囲の景観に溶け込んでいる。(オーバーアマガウ)

A town in southern Germany with the Alps mountains in the background. Black and yellow are cleverly used, giving off a clean, warm, and airy impression. The red and green dots are also set off, and the colors of the traffic signals also blend in with the surrounding scenery (Oberammergau)

## 景観の公共性

　まちは市民のひとりひとりに喜びと希望を与え，その
まちに住んでよかったという，生活に対する配慮をもっ
て創りあげていこうとする思想が生まれている。それは
個人の恣意を無制限に実現するというのではなく，まち
全体を活性化させながら調和がとれたまちにしていこう
とする機運が高まっているからである。そうしたことの
一つの表れとして，街路の景観に及ぼす屋外広告物の影
響を考え，制限する方向に向かっている。

　私的な表示は私的空間や敷地内に限るのが原則である。
道路から見えるものについてもその大きさや表現方法を
制限する方向にある。従来自治体の財源難によって一部
の構築物に協賛広告を入れたケースもあったが，公共的
な品位を損なうという観点から次第に姿を消しつつある。
今後は一層その方向へ向かうに違いない。

**Publicness of Scenes**

　　　A new idea has appeared which regards
community planning as to give joy and hope to
individual citizens as well as a sense of fulfillment and
satisfaction of living in the community. It is not an
intention to meet all the desires of the individuals but a
thought to create a whole community as to be an
active and harmoneous place to live in. One example
can be found in the movement of restriction of the
outdoor advertisements with considerations to their
influence on the street scene.

　　　Some cities have limited the private signs only
to the private site and those that can be seen from the
streets to certain sizes and restricted expressions.
There used to be the cases that the regional
administrations put advertisements of sponsorship on
the buildings due to their financial shortage, but they
gradually disappear according to the recognition that
they ruine publicness. Such a tendency will be
accelerated from now on.

1975年頃の日本では他人の家の壁面に無造作に広告
が貼られたりしていた。

It was quite common around 1975 to see posters
and advertisements carelessly placed on the
walls of privates homes in Japan.

1975年頃の日本の街路。乱雑に置かれた袖看板や立
て看板。電柱の広告。公道からこうした広告は追放
したいものである。

Streets of Japan around 1975. Disorderly signs
and advertisements on telephone poles. We
would like to banish such advertisements from
public roads.

気になる自動販売機。この例は敷地内に収まってい
るが歩道にはみ出しているものが多い。何らかの規
制を考えねばならぬ時期に来ているのではなかろう
か。

A vending machine. Although this example
shows the machine within the grounds, many
protrude onto the sidewalk. It has become necessary to consider some form of regulations for
such situations.

福岡市はバス停のベンチから広告を除き，公共空間の位置付けを明確にした。

The city of Fukuoka has removed all advertisements from bus stop benches, making the position of public space clear.

ミラノ大聖堂の広場をはさんだ向かい側の壁がネオンで埋まっている。その大半が日本企業であり，かなり批判されている。

The wall across from the square in front of the Cathedral of Milano is covered with neon signs. Most are those of Japanese businesses, and have been greatly criticized.

工事現場や空き地のフェンスにも景観上の配慮をして企業のイメージアップを図る例が現われてきた。

We are seeing more examples in which consideration is given to the scenery when building fences around construction sites and vacant lots, in an attempt to improve the firm's image.

# 屋外広告物のコントロール

　屋外広告物とは，ポスター，張り紙，のぼり，懸垂幕，立看板，暖簾，店舗の看板，広告板，広告塔，ネオンサインなど，営利と宣伝を目的にすると否とにかかわらず，名前や標語なども含めた屋外で表示したり設置するすべての表示物のことである。

　屋外広告は建物や町並みのイメージを形成する一部であり，景観を創りあげるうえで非常に重要である。そこで景観整備の一環としてこれを規制する事例が増えつつある。一般に規制する地域の細分化，規制内容の強化，すぐれたデザインの奨励が行われている。

　1）面積と高さの制限

　都市によって若干の違いはあるが，広告物の高さや面積は条例によって規制されている。「屋外広告物」は高さを建物の 3 分の 2 以内とする例が大半で，地域によって違いがあり，面積は10㎡から100㎡以下にする例が多い。「袖看板広告」ははとんどが20㎡以下で，歩道上2.5～3.5 m 以上，車道上4.5～4.7m 以上に取り付けるようにするなどまちまちに規制されている。「広告板」や「広告塔」は面積10㎡から100㎡までとこれもまちまちに規制されている。これらの規制が緩いのではないかという批判も多い。

　屋外広告物はまちの賑わいを演出する効果もある。しかし，際限のない競争によって，大きいことが必ずしも効果的ではないという反省を経て，今日ではデザインの質が求められる時代になっている。こうした点を踏まえてその地域の特性や性格に応じた，きめ細かい対応が必要であろう。

　2）色彩の制限

　一般的に色彩について強制的な制限は設けられていないが，赤，黄色，などの派手な純色を避け，色数を制限するように行政指導しているところが多いようである。蛍光色や反射塗料の使用を制限しているところもある。新しい方法として彩度による面積の制限を試行しているところもある。

　3）照明とサイン

　美観地区に指定されている一部の地区や地域において，ネオンサインやイルミネーションなどが禁止されているところもあるが，一般的に強い規制をしているところは少ない。大都市の一部は夜間の活動が活発となっており，夜間の景観の形成を考えた規制を考えねばならないところにきているようである。

　4）形状

　公衆への危険防止のため，4m を越えるものについては構造計算書の添付が必要である。ボストンではデザイン内容まで行政指導によって制限しているが，日本ではそこまで踏み込むのは難しく，今後の課題として残されている。

# 屋外広告物の大きさと範囲の制限

　屋外広告は大きいほど注目度が高いと考えられ，大きさを競った時代があったが，その競争の結果かえって逆効果になるとして，最近では所と場所に応じた適正なサイズに落ち着いてきたようである。まちの景観が，広告物の氾濫で台なしになっているところもあり，今後の都市景観や美観の上から壁面の利用と安全，景観の面からもこれをどの程度にするか，行政，都市計画者，建築家，広告物制作者らの間の活発な意見交換と討議を期待したい。

商店街が雑然としているのは日本だけではない。街路を限定してにぎわいを演出する要素として看板を効果的に設けることも考えられる。

Japan is not the only country in which shopping streets are disorderly. One way of producing an element of gaiety by limiting the streets is to effectively place signs.

**Control of Outdoor Advertisements**

　　　Outdoor advertisements are all kinds of signs placed or displayed outdoor including names and phrases, whether for the sake of profits and publicity or not.

　　　Outdoor advertisements are a part of creating an image of buildings and communities, and are very important in planning scenes. Cases of restriction of the outdoor advertisements are increasing as a part of the scene planning. Generally, the subdivision of the region, stricter regulations and good designs are recommended.

1) Restrictions of area and height

　　　The height and area of an advertisement are decided in the regulations with slight differences according to cities. The contents of the regulations vary in regions, but most of them set the height under two-thirds of that of the building and the area from 10 to 100 square meters. Signboards are mostly under 20 square meters and should be displayed 2.5 to 3.5 meters high above a sidewalk and 4.5 to 4.7 meters high above a street. The regulations for signboards and signtowers vary from 10 to 100 square meters, but they are criticized for insufficient restrictions.

　　　Outdoor advertisements are also effective in creating the atmosphere of the city. According to experience in the past large advertisements are not necessarily effective because of the competitions to make unlimitedly big signs or piling them up on the roofs. Nowadays the quality of the design is demanded. With those points in mind, detailed considerations will be needed based on the regional character.

2) Restriction of color

　　　There are not coersive restrictions in terms of a color generally, but there are administrative guidance to avoid showy colors such as red and yellow and to limit the number of colors used in the advertisement. Others also restrict the use of fluorescent paints or reflex paints. Restriction of chrome is also under consideration in some cases.

3) Lights and signs

　　　There are not strict restrictions in terms of lights generally except in some areas and districts designated as regions of scenic beauty where neon lamps and illuminations are inhibited. Night time becomes more and more active in some large cities and it seems to be the time to think of regulations for the night scene planning.

4) Form

　　　A structual accounting form is required for those over 4-meter-high due to prevention of the danger to the public. Even the content of the design is restricted by administrative guidance in Boston, but the same is difficult in Japan and remains as a future subject.

**Regulation of size and Extent of Outdoor Advertisements**

　　　There was a time of competing the size in the past with an idea that larger an outdoor advertisement is, greater attention it can draw. But now based on a thought that such a competion leads to a counter result it seems to have calmed down to a proper size in a proper place. Some cities are ruined their scenes by the over-advertisements. Active discussions among architects and PR producers on the use of the walls from the perspectives of beauty as well as of safety and the extent are highly expected.

看板の規制が厳しいハイデルベルグのマクドナルドは，小さな看板しか出していないが，かえって効果的である。

The McDonald's in Heidelberg, a city with strict regulations regarding signs, is small but effective.

東京・渋谷の例。シュミレーションとして看板を消してみると建物の存在感がなくなることがわかる。

Example in Shibuya, Tokyo. When the scene is simulated and the signs removed, the buildings lose their sense of existence.

競いあって大きな看板を取りつけがちだが、景観との調和を考慮していく必要がある。

Although firms often compete in the size of signs, preferring large ones, it is necessary to pay attention to the relationship between them and the surrounding scenery, as well.

屋外広告が二階までに押さえられた例。低層部は賑
やかで楽しい歩行空間がつくられている。高層部は
広告物がないので建物の特徴が見え、都市全体のス
カイラインが美しくなる。

An example in which outdoor advertising is
limited to the second floor. A gay and fun walking
space has been created on the lower level. Since
the upper level has no advertisements, the building's characteristics are visible, making a beautiful city skyline.

イベント時は思い切った楽しさの演出が効果的で、
規制を緩和する。

Daring displays of joy and happiness are effective
during events, softening regulations.

商業空間では派手な色彩が賑わいを演出しているこ
ともある。場所に応じたコントロールを考えていか
ねばならない。

Bright colors are often used to produce gaiety in
commercial spaces. It is necessary to control
colors according to the place.

## 広告物デザインの質

　わが国は漢字文化圏であり，識字能力も高いところから，屋外広告物も文字に頼る傾向が強かった。その名残りは今でも暖簾や木製の看板などに残っており，それなりの風情がある。近年，経済性，均一性，大量生産などの理由に加え，夜間営業のために合成樹脂の内照式看板が一般化した。個性や味わい，親しみやすさを考えると，素材，建造物や周辺のイメージなどにマッチしたデザインを再発掘すべき時にきていると思う。

　広告物のデザインの質を高めるには，シンポジウムや表彰制度などによる啓蒙活動が欠かせない。設計の現場，制作者の感性を育てることも必要であり，一般市民の美意識をそそり，まち全体が美しいまとまりを形成していくための継続的な研究や講習も必要であろう。

### Quality of Design of Advertisements

　　Outdoor advertisements tended to depend on letters because Japanese culture is based on Chinese characters and thus a literacy rate is high. They can still be found in wooden signboards today and show good old days. Today signs made of synthetic resins are seen everywhere which also function as lights at night. It is time to explore designs to match the materials and a sense of beauty in order to express distinctive characters and familiality.

　　Symposiums and awards will be helpful to raise the quality of the design of advertisements. It is also necessary to foster senses of those who work at the construction site. Continuous study and schooling are also mandatory towards the aim that a community creates a beautiful totality and inspires the sense of beauty of the public.

シュバビッシャル

Schwäbisch Hall

リンブルク

Limburg

まちの楽しさを演出する道具だてになっている袖看板。具象的な例が多く，デザインの質も高い。
アーヘン

Signs used as tools to produce the gaiety of the town. Many examples are figurative, and the level of design is high.
Aachen

ロンドン。ユニークな絵看板が多い。

London. There are many unique picture signs.

東京・銀座の伊東屋の小粋なサイン。

Stylish sign of Itoya, a shop in Ginza, Tokyo.

直接的な店名の表示以外の方法で注目を集める。

An example of gaining attention by using signs indicating not only the shop's name.

メーアスブルグ

Meersburg

資生堂，ザ・ギンザの小型サイン。芸術的水準の高
さを感じさせる。

Small sign of Shiseido's "The Ginza" store. The
artistic level is very high.

数寄屋橋の角にあるソニービルは三角形の空間を公
共のものとして考え，いろんな催事を行っている。
今では世界的に有名な情報の発信スペースになって
いる。

The Sony building on the corner of Sukiyabashi,
Tokyo. The triangular space is considered to be
public, and many events are held here. It is now
famous around the world as being a space for
data transmission.

西武百貨店のお正月のディスプレイ。新年にふさわ
しい演出である。

New Year's display at the Seibu Department
Store. It is appropriate for this special time of
year.

完成度の高いデザイン。

A highly perfected design.

日本の伝統的な情緒を感じさせる暖簾。

Shop curtain conveying a traditional Japanese
atmosphere.

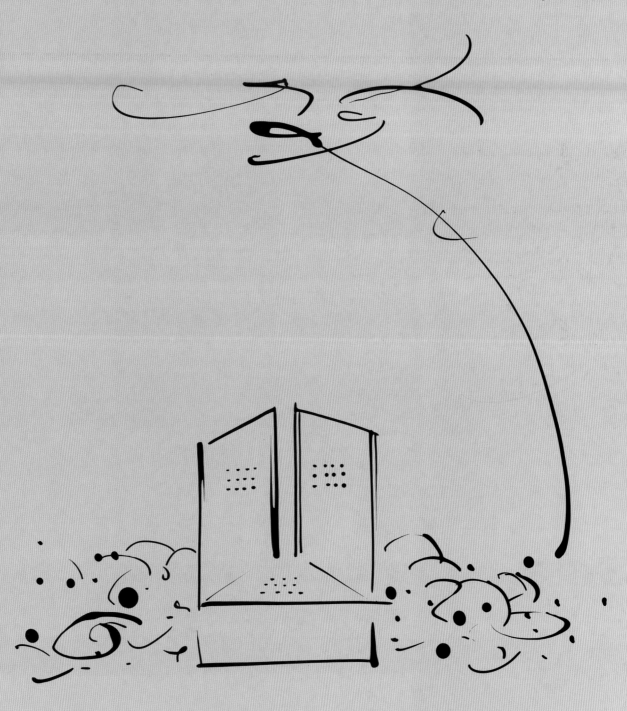

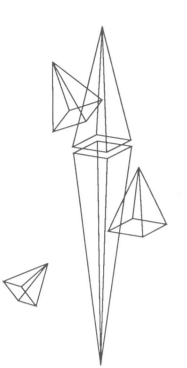

# 1.まちづくりとサイン計画

## City Planning and Signs

まちのイメージアップを図る手段として「サイン」が注目され、サイン計画が各地で行われている。サインはまちの情報を的確に伝え活性化を図る一つの方法として取り上げられている。これは地域にあるさまざまな資源を、住民に理解してもらい、確認する手段としても有効である。

サインはさまざまな情報を伝える「記号」を意味し、標識や看板のような表示物だけでなく、ランドマークや身振り手振りや信号音など、意志を伝達したり意味を伝える多様な記号全般のことである。

昔から地域で親しまれてきた大きな樹木やお地蔵さんのように、本来の意味の他に目印として、またそれにまつわるエピソードを伝えるサインとしての役割を果たすものもある。

自治体などの公共的な機関が設置するサインは「公共サイン」であり、公共サインは公共施設、公共空間、公共の物件などの所在を明らかにし、機能をわかりやすく説明する。サインは伝えたい内容を基準化することによって、正確で信頼性が増し、安定した情報の伝達を行う機能をもっている。

ランドマークとしてよく使われるオベリスク。(エウル)

An obelisk, often used as a landmark. (E.U.R.)

Many cities are making "sign planning" responding to the growing interest in "signs" as a means to improve the image of cities. Signs are now regarded as a method to transmit correctly information related to cities and invigorate urban life. Signs are also an effective means to have city dwellers understand and recognize the situation and facts about resources existing in their cities.

Signs are a "symbol" which transmits various kinds of information. Signs are not merely things which are put up for attracting the public attention, such as signboards, but they are also symbols shown in a variety of forms, like gestures and signals which transmit intentions and meanings.

In some areas, there have been huge trees and stone-carved images of Jizo (guardian deity) which inhabitants there have been looking up to, for many years, with a fond feeling. Similar to this, some signs fulfill their roles as landmarks for urbanites and as transmitters of episodes connected with these objects, besides their original role as signs.

Public signs put up by local autonomous entities and public organs show the locations of public facilitie, space areas and buildings. They also tell in an easy-to-understand way what functions these establishments have. One function of signs is to transmit unmistakable information, by standardizing the contents of information and by thus giving it authenticity and trustworthiness.

東京・浅草の雷門。まち全体のイメージを象徴している。

The "Kaminari-mon" gate in Asakusa, Tokyo. It symbolizes the entire town's image.

# サインが伝える情報

　サインによって伝えられる情報を整理して考えれば，おおよそ次の通りに分類できる。

1）空間情報
　　1－1）案内
　　　　空間の構成を示す面的情報
　　　　　例：地図，配置図
　　1－2）誘導
　　　　方向や行先を示す線的情報
　　　　　例：方向案内
　　1－3）記名
　　　　場所を特定する点的情報
　　　　　例：町名街区番号，表札

2）運営情報
　　2－1）制御
　　　　安全管理と利用の円滑化
　　　　　例：注意，禁止，指示
　　2－2）解説
　　　　内容の説明，紹介，理解の促進
　　　　　例：利用案内，使用説明，学習
　　2－3）掲示
　　　　臨時や随時の可変的情報の表示
　　　　　例：掲示板，伝言板，旗

3）広告
　　　認知の拡大や説得を目的とした情報
　　　　例：屋上広告，袖看板広告

## Signs Transmit Information

Information transmitted by signs can be grouped as follows:
1) Information on Space Areas
　1-1) Guidances
　　Information on space areas which show the composition of plane space
　　Examples:　Maps; arrangement plans
　1-2) Directions
　　Information which uses lines for showing directions and destinations
　　Examples:　Guidances on directions
　1-3) Signs
　　Information shown by points; it specifies spots
　　Examples:　The names of towns and blocs; numbers given to places; doorplates
2) Operational Information
　2-1) Control
　　Safety control and the facilitation of use
　　Examples:　Caution; prohibitions; directions
　2-2) Explanations
　　Explanations and PR on contents; the promotion of understanding
　　Examples:　Guidances on usage; explanations on ways to use them; studies on how to use
　2-3) Notices
　　Providing of temporary and occasional information
　　Examples:　Notice boards; message boards; flags
3) Advertisements
　　Information aimed at prompting recognition and facilitating persuasion
　　Examples:　Rooftop advertisements; signboards placed on the ground

# 伝える対象

1）歩行者
　　歩行者にとって必要な情報。歩行または立ち止まって利用するもの。
2）自転車
　　自転車にとって必要な情報。安全な走行のための情報や，サイクリング道路などの専用道路で表示する情報。
3）自動車
　　自動車にとって必要な情報。走行状態で利用する。利用者は自動車に限定され，道路の状況に応じて，すみやかな情報の伝達が必要である。
4）障害者
　　障害者にとって必要な情報。障害者のために特別に設けるもの。

## Objects of Information

1) Pedestrians
　Information for pedestrians; information seen by them while walking or information which they look at by standing still
2) Bicyclists
　Information for bicyclists; information for safe cycling and information shown in cycling parks, especially in cycling paths and bicycle lanes
3) Automobile Drivers
　Information for auto drivers; they use information while driving; information exclusively intended for auto drivers; it is necessary to supply information promptly on highway situations
4) Physically Handicapped Persons
　Information for handicapped persons; information specially designed for use by these persons

## Classification of Information

1) Signs in Towns
　Signs as the guide of towns
2) Housing-Connected Signs
　Signs concerning housing and living
3) Signs in Parks
　Signs related to the maintenance, control and management of parks
4) Information on Traffic
　Signs related to automobiles, public transportation facilities, etc.
5) Commercial Business Signs
　Signs concerning commercial activities
6) Signs for Public Facilities
　Signs for individual public facilities
7) Landmarks
　Individual signs, such as symbols, marks, monuments, carvings and engravings, etc.

# サインの種類

1）都市系サイン
　　都市を案内するサイン。
2）住宅系サイン
　　住居や生活に関するサイン。
3）公園系サイン
　　公園の維持，管理，運営に関するサイン。
4）交通サイン
　　自動車，公共的交通機関などに関するサイン。
5）商業系サイン
　　商業活動に関するサイン。
6）施設系サイン
　　個別の施設に関するサイン。
7）ランドマーク
　　シンボル，目印，記念碑，彫刻など個別のサイン。

近代化された都市サイン。情報の集約，地図の充実，見やすさ，道具としての質感などが向上している。（福岡市）

A modernized city sign. The intensity of data, completeness of maps, comprehensiveness, and quality as a tool are improving. (Fukuoka City)

日常的な情報の変化にも対応しようとしたサイン。（マインツ）

This sign attempts to cope with the daily changes of data. (Mainz)

地図の部分拡大。情報をわかりやすく序列化した。英文併記が一般化してきた。（福岡市）

Enlarged section of a map. Data has been displayed in an order easily comprehended. It is now common to include explanations in English, as well. (Fukuoka City)

施設のサイン：施設の特性に似合った形態を吟味すれば、雰囲気も伝えられる。

Facility signs: It is possible to convey the atmosphere by examining a form suiting the facility's characteristics.

交通サイン：パリ地下鉄の路線案内はパリらしい芸術と文化の薫りがするすぐれたデザインである。（フランス）

Transportation sign: The design of the route map of the Paris subway system is excellent, having an air of art and culture suiting this city.

素材や表現方法は多様で、独創的な形がある。（東京・数寄屋橋）

Materials and forms of expression are diverse, with creative style. (Sukiyabashi, Tokyo)

ピクトグラムだけで簡潔に誘導する例。利用者が多い施設の経路を示す場合に有効な方法である。

An example concisely guiding people using only pictograms. It is an effective method in displaying routes in facilities that are used by many people.

日本の伝統的な石の誘導サイン。交通標識の設置場所や景観との調和についての配慮が今後の課題だ。

A traditional Japanese stone guiding sign. The main topic to consider from now on is the location of the sign, as well as the harmony between the sign and the surrounding scenery.

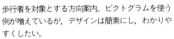

歩行者を対象とする方向案内。ピクトグラムを使う例が増えているが、デザインは簡素にし、わかりやすくしたい。

Direction information for pedestrians. Pictograms are being used increasingly. The design should be concise and easily comprehensible.

清楚なまちを印象づける自然石と木による美しい誘導サイン。（オブストドルフ）

A beautiful guiding sign made of natural stone and wood, emphasizing this neat town. (Oberstdorf)

交通標識を地域の誘導サインに組み込んだ例。狭い場所を効率的に使うよう苦心している。

An example of traffic signs incorporated into local guiding signs. The major concern here is how to utilize the limited space most efficiently.

自動車向けの行先誘導サイン。低い位置で小さいが、設置された場所が適切であればわかりやすい。

A sign to guide cars in the right direction. Even if the sign is small and low, if the location is appropriate. It is easily comprehensible.

モーゼル河畔の小さなまちで見かけたサインだが、合理的でありながら人の心に訴えるものがある。

A sign found in a small town along the Moselle River. Although functional, it also appeals to the human emotions.

トイレの誘導。ヨーロッパではこうした表現を多く見かける。

Guiding sign for restroom. Such methods of expression are common in Europe.

天然石を使った誘導サイン。素材の温もりが伝わってくる。

A guiding sign using natural stone. We can feel the warmth of the material.

施設内の誘導サイン。とくにあわただしい空港などでは、心が和らぐ表現が欲しい。

A guiding sign within a facility. It is especially necessary to use peaceful expressions in busy facilities such as airports.

沖縄海洋博記念公園のトイレ誘導。位置は低いが探しやすく適確な表示である。

Guiding signs for restrooms at the Okinawa Ocean Exposition Memorial National Government Park. Although placed low, they are easily found, and the directions are accurate.

まちの中心街での誘導。派手でモダンなデザインだが簡潔な表現となっている。建物ともマッチしている。

A sign guiding people in the center of town. Although the design is bold and modern, the expression is concise. The sign also matches the buildings.

まちで見かけたトイレの誘導。絵柄から昔の生活の様子が偲ばれる。距離が表示されているのは親切だ。

Sign for restrooms in a city. The pictures express what life used to be like. Concidaration is shown by displaying distances, as well.

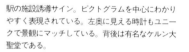

駅の施設誘導サイン。ピクトグラムを中心にわかりやすく表現されている。左奥に見える時計もユニークで景観にマッチしている。背後は有名なケルン大聖堂である。

A facility guiding sign of a station. The meaning is easily comprehended when the pictogram's design is clear.
The clock seen in the background is unique, and matches its surroundings. The great cathedral of Cologne is seen in the background.

観光地にある古城のトイレ誘導。周辺の環境にも配慮している。

A sign guiding visitors to the restrooms in an old castle, now a popular tourist site. The surroundings have been taken into con- sideration.

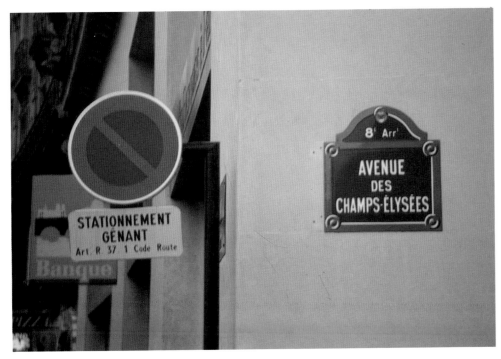

パリの地点記名。事務的な標識にもパリらしさを表現しようとしている。

Signs showing the names of places in Paris. An attempt has been made to express the feeling of the city even in such practical signs.

観光名所の記名。石に彫刻を施しているが, 小さくても気が利いたサインになっている。

Inscriptions of tourist sites. The names are engraved in stone, and although quite small, the design is clever and attractive.

目についた美しいデザインの記名サイン。質の高いデザインの集積は, まちの品格を高めていく。

An beautiful inscription that came to our attention. The accumulation of high-grade designs increases the refinement of the city.

停留所のサイン。すぐれたデザインと色彩が目に止まった。(チューリッヒ)

A bus stop sign: We noticed the excellent design and colors. (Zurich)

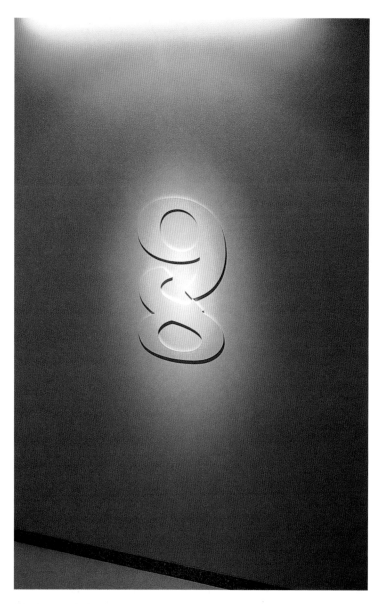

東京・銀座伊東屋の階数表示。洗練されたデザイン
とアイデアで表現力も豊かである。

Floor indications for the Itoya, a shop in Ginza,
Tokyo. The refined design and ideas make it an
expressive display.

絵文字でまちを表現したユニークなゲート。そこに
住む人たちの優しい気持ちが伝わってくる。

A unique gate expressing the town using pic-
togrms. The warmth of the people living there is
conveyed.

路面電車の表示。緊張感があるいいデザインだ。

A streetcar display. The design is tense and
excellent.

ロンドンの動物園のサインの制御サイン。周囲にも
配慮したデザインで，6カ国語が記載されている。
世界中から人が集まってくる英国ならではである。

Control signs in a London zoo. The design takes
into consideration the surrounding scenery, with
instructions given in six languages. This is neces
sary in the U.K., since people visit here from
around the world.

よく見かける注意サインだが，景観に配慮したい。

This is a typical caution sign. More attention
should be paid to the surrounding scenery.

制御サインの基本。人による交通制御。腕の動かし
方に約束がある。立っているブースのデザインもい
い。

The basic control sign. Traffic control by people.
The design of the booth is also attractive.

ペット用のトイレを案内するサイン。遊び心を心得
たサインである。

A sign showing the location of a pet toilet. The
designer understands the need for some humor
in such signs.

読ませる工夫をした巧みなサイン。地域の環境にも
調和している。表現も適切だ。

A clever sign encouraging people to read it. It is in
harmony with its surroundings, and the expressions are appropriate, as well.

人の立小便禁止のサイン。神社の鳥居をマークする
ことによって防ごうとするもので，日本では古くか
ら使われてきた。(京都)

A sign prohibiting men from urinating in public.
The sign of a shrine's gate has been used traditionally in Japan for this purpose.

物理的に制限する方法は，感情的な抵抗感がすくない。

Methods regulating physically have less emotional resistance.

進入禁止のサイン。表現がおだやかで好感をもって迎えられている。(静岡県・掛川市)

A "No Entry" sign. The expression is tranquil, and is quite popular. (Kakegawa City, Shizuoka Prefecture)

動物学習サイン。目の前にいる動物を学習できる効
果がある。(海の中道海浜公園)

Animal study signs. Visitors are able to study
about the animals in front of them. (Umino-
nakamichi Seaside National Government Park)

動物園の学習サイン。動物の特徴を図で解説し、一
歩踏み込んだ詳しい説明をする親切さがある。(ロン
ドン)

Animal study signs in a zoo. The animals' characteristics are described with drawings, with
detailed descriptions given. (London)

由布院駅のダイヤ表示。列車の運行がコンパクトに
まとめられている。利用者が少ない駅ではこうした
表示が便利である。

The train schedule is compactly displayed at
Yufuin Station. Such displays are convenient in
stations with few passengers.

秋月のサイン。自然との一体感がある。

Signs in Akizuki-machi. Unity has been formed
with nature.

施設内の総合掲示。常に新しい情報を提供できる。
（ロンドン動物園）

A facility's composite display. New data is continuously being provided. (London Zoo)

シャンゼリゼで賛否両論が起こり話題となった電光掲示板。大型で景観にそぐわぬという批判があったが，洗練された完成度が高いデザインである。

The electric bulletin board on Les Champs-Elysees that gained attention for the discussions on its pros and cons. Although there was concern that it was too large and harmed the scenery, the design is refined and of high quality.

壁面の利用。すぐれた描画のテクニックでアクティブで洗練された印象を与えている。

Using a wall. Excellent painting techniques given an active and refined impression.

ヨーロッパの伝統的な広告塔。日本ではこの種の広告塔は設置場所の選択と維持管理が難しいであろう。

A traditional European advertisement tower. Such towers would be difficult in Japan in terms of selection of location and maintenance.

ユニークな掲示板。立体的なものも掲示できるようになっている。

A unique bulletin board. It is possible to display cubic images, as well.

## さまざまな表現方法

1）小工作物による表現
　　一般的な独立した物によるサイン。大小の工作物，
　　自立したものや何か別のものに付帯するものなど。

2）建築物による表現
　　建築にサイン的な効果を持たせたもの。色彩や素材，
　　壁画の意匠，建物自体を象徴的に個性化するなど。

3）造園修景物による表現
　　造園的な手法によってサイン性を発揮させるもの。
　　地面の整形や植物，照明などの修景物を活用するな
　　ど。

4）土木構築物による表現
　　土地利用や大規模なランドスケープ。動線や起伏な
　　どの視覚的な変化を計画的に演出したり，活用した
　　りする。

5）自然物による表現
　　自然の表情の活用。自然景観のクローズアップ，季
　　節の変化，動植物とのふれあいなどを印象づける。

### Various Methods of Representation

1) Representations Using Small-size Manufactured
   Objects
   Signs using one individual object; large and small
   manufactured objects; objects which are singly used
   as signs; objects attached to some other objects
2) Representations Using Buildings
   Buildings which have effects similar to signs; colors;
   materials; designs of mural paintings; buildings built
   as symbolically characteristic buildings
3) Representations with the aid of landscaping
   Those which display the characteristics of signs by
   using garden design techniques; they include the
   remodeling of the ground and the utilization of
   plants, lighting and other scenic objects
4) Representation Using Engineering Construction
   Techniques
   Using of land and grand landscape; to use scenic
   changes, such as the lines of flow and undulations
   for the creation of visual effects
5) Representation Using Nature
   Using of phenomenon shown by nature; close-up of
   natural scenic beauty; to highlight seasonal
   changes; man's contact with nature

小工作物による最も一般的な表現。個性化を図り発
想を広げて考えることが大切である。

The most common method of expression, using
small handicraft items. It is important to be creative and imaginative.

建築物による表現。形態を象徴的に扱ったり，建物
の表面を個性的にしたり，一時的に装飾を施すなど
いろいろな方法がある。

Expressions through the use of architectural
structures. Many methods are available, such as
treating the form abstractly, designing unique
surfaces, or temporarily decorating the building.

造園的な手法によって道や空間に特別な意味を持たせた例。

An example in which roads and spaces have been given special meaning through the use of landscaping techniques.

土木構築物による表現例。ユニークな空間の設定でまちの個性が強く印象づけられる。

An example of expression using public works structures. The city's characteristics are stressed by setting a unique space.

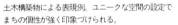

造園的な手法によって経路を示す。

It is possible to use landscaping methods to indicate the route.

造園修景物による表現。トイレや茶室を暗示する日本の伝統的な表現。

Expressions using landscaping objects. Traditional Japanese expressions suggesting restrooms and tea-ceremony rooms.

美しい自然物による表現。ライン河とモーゼル河が合流する「ドイツの角」と呼ばれる観光ポイント。

An expression using beautiful items from nature. The point at which the Moselle and Rhine Rivers meet is a famous tourist site called the "Corner of Germany."

## サイン計画の手順
## PROCESS FOR SIGN PLANNING

| | | |
|---|---|---|
| 調査・基本構想<br>RESEARCH<br>PLANNING | 現状・問題・事例調査<br>理念・方針の検討<br>サイン計画の事業化 | SITUATION,PROBLEM,CASE STUDY<br>DISCUSSION FOR POLICY,AIM<br>ORDER TO PROJECT |
| 基本設計<br>FUNDAMENTAL<br>DESIGN | 対象・範囲・手段の計画<br>情報の構成<br>デザインコンセプト策定<br>表示基本設計<br>構造基本設計<br>配置基本計画 | PLANNING ON OBJECT, AREA, METHOD<br>INFORMATION COMPOSITION<br>DESIGN CONCEPT<br>VISUAL FORMAT DESIGN<br>STRUCTURE STANDARD ITEMS DESIGN<br>POSITIONING STANDARD PLANNIGN |
| 実施設計<br>PRACTICAL DESIGN | 表示実施設計<br>構造実施設計<br>配置実施設計 | VISUAL DESIGN<br>STRUCTURE DESIGN<br>POSITIONING DESIGN |
| 製作・施工<br>PRODUCTION | 表示部製作<br>構造部製作<br>施工・設置 | VISUAL PARTS PRODUCT<br>STRUCTURE PARTS PRODUCT<br>CONSTRUCTION, SET UP |
| 維持管理<br>MAINTENANCE | 定期点検・清掃<br>修理・更新 | CHECK, CLEANING<br>REPAIRING, RENEWAL |

アイデアの検討。情報内容や形態などの表現を考える。

Evaluation of the idea. Expressions of the data content and form are evaluated.

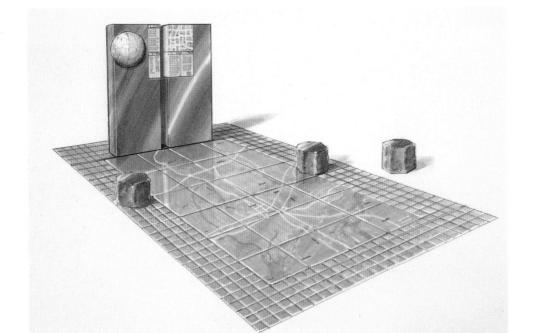

実施案の検討。ミニモデルやパースなどによって具体化する案を考え，形態，素材，仕上げ，価格などを検討する。

Working plan. Concrete ideas are considered using miniature models and perspectives. The form, materials, finish, and price are evaluated.

## サイン計画の留意点

　サインを計画するに当たっては，伝えたい情報を内容に応じて次のように整理しておくと的確な表現となる。

1）伝達性

　　伝えたい情報を的確に選択し構成する。その目的を明確にし表現が適切であること。

2）使用性

　　見やすく使いやすいこと。耐久性にすぐれ，維持管理が容易であること。製作コストやランニングコストが適当であること。

3）物質性

　　安全で安定した生産ができること。信頼性があり，品質がよいこと。情報が明瞭に表現されていて，簡潔でわかりやすいこと。

4）情緒性

　　美しさ，楽しさ，品位があること。形，素材，色などの印象が良く，親しみやすく，人々に好感がもたれるもの。

5）連続性

　　他の造形物との表現の一貫性があること。周辺環境の将来構想と調和し連続性があること。周囲の協力が得られ，長期的な継続性があること。

6）個性

　　環境や文化の特徴を的確に解釈し，リードするものであること。独創的で話題性があること。今後の発展が期待できること。

### Points to Be Noted in Drawing up Signs

If the contents of the information to be transmitted are arranged as follows, before drawing up plans for signs, it will become possible to use accurate expressions.

1) Transmission

Select and compose accurately the information to be transmitted. Show the purpose of the information clearly and use proper expressions.

2) Usage

It should be easy to look at signs, and the use thereof should be easy. They should be highly durable and easy to maintain and control. Production and running costs should be reasonable.

3) Materials

Use materials which are safe and capable of creating well-balanced products. They should be dependable and of high quality. Information should be clearly presented. It should be clear-cut, and also easy to understand.

4) Emotions

Beauty, fun, and refinement. Objects that give favorable and warm impressions in terms of shape, material, and color.

5) Continuity

Must have consistency in expression with other structures. Must harmonize with future plans for the surrounding environment, and have a sense of continuity. The cooperation of others must be available, and have long-term continuity.

6) Individuality

The characteristics of the environment and culture must be clearly interpreted, and the object should act as a leader. The object must be unique and become a topic of conversation. Future development must be expected.

原寸モデルによる現場検討。予算やスケジュールに余裕がある場合は原寸モデルをつくって実施案のチェックをするとよい。

The site is evaluated using actual size models. When there is time and money to spare, actual size models should be made to check the working plan.

完成。正しく製作・設置されていることを確認する。その後定期点検，清掃，補修修理，補充，更新などを行う。

Finish. Confirm that production and placement are accurate. Periodical inspections, cleaning, repairs, supplements, and renewal then become necessary.

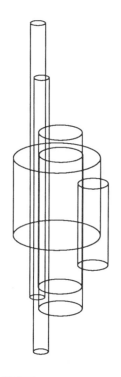

# 2.まちの情報のデザイン化
## Designing Town's Information

直接的な方向案内は，誘導する対象が少ない場合は効果的だが，多いとかえって理解しにくくなる。

Direct guidance instructions are effective when the objects of guidance are few, but when this is not the case, they become difficult to comprehend.

## 誘導計画
## Guiding Plans

案内誘導の方法は，大きく分けて方向案内やラインによって，個別に行先を指示するリニア誘導型，特徴のある目印によって位置関係を確認するランドマーク誘導型，地図を主体とした地図誘導型などがある。

1）リニア誘導型

リニア誘導型は個別の施設などを連続的に誘導する方法で，利用頻度が高い目的地を示すために有効である。また瞬間的に方向を知らせることができる。しかし，誘導する対象が限定され，何を強調すべきかをあらかじめ決めておく必要がある。トイレや救護所やインフォメーションなどの利用頻度や緊急性の高い施設については，リニア誘導が適切である。

2）ランドマーク誘導型

ランドマーク誘導型は，彫刻などの目印を中心にして誘導する方法で，最近の博覧会や駅の待合せなどにも利用されている。親しみやすくわかりやすい。とくに繁雑な空間では効果的な方法である。

3）地図誘導型

地図誘導型は地図を確認しながら誘導する方法で，都市や住宅環境や各種施設などで一般的に使われている。多様な目的地を任意に検索でき，相対的な位置関係を把握することができる。地図はわかりやすく美しい表現とし，現場で照合しやすくする。

There are roughly three ways to give guidance: The linear guiding method of showing destinations by using lines; the landmark guiding method of confirming positions by looking at eye-catching marks; and the map guiding method.

1) Linear Guiding Method

This method is used when the locations of more than one individual facilities standing in continuous series are shown. This method is effective in shown the directions of buildings that are frequented. Also, this method enables viewers to confirm in a moment the directions of the buildings they are looking for. However, the objects to be shown by this method are limited. It is therefore necessary to decide in advance on which buildings stress should be placed. The linear guiding method is most suitable for showing the directions of toilets, first-aid stations and information offices which are very frequently used in an emergency.

2) Landmark Guiding Method

The landmark guiding method is a method which shows directions by pointing to sculptures and other objects that attract viewers' attention. This method has come to be used at exhibition sites, waiting rooms in stations, etc. This method, which is easy to understand, is especially effective when used for showing destinations in crowded places.

3) Map Guiding Method

The map guiding method is the method to find directions through the use of maps. The method is generally used in cities, residential areas, at various facilities, etc. By using this method, viewers can check voluntarily into diversified destinations, and grasp inter-relations between destinations. Maps should be drawn up so that they will be easy to look up, and pleasant designs should be used.

1）リニア誘導型
Linear Guidance Method

リニア誘導は，線的に個別の施設などの方向を表わす方法。観光地などでは矢印だけの単純な誘導でもルートが理解しやすい。ただし矢印には行動を強制する意味があるので設置場所に注意する。

The linear method uses lines to express the direction of individual facilities and so forth. In tourist sites it is possible to give clear instructions by simply using arrows. However, since arrows indicate enforced activity, it is necessary to be careful in deciding where to place them.

行動の分岐点では簡潔で正確な方向指示が必要である。

Concise and accurate direction instructions are necessary at junctions of activities.

2) ランドマーク誘導型
Landmark Guiding Method

まちの新しいランドマークとなった福岡タワー。

The Fukuoka Tower has become the city's new landmark.

バイオリンづくりの町，ミッテンバルトの彫刻。

The sculptures of Mittenwald, a town famous for violin making.

通行人にときどき水を吹きかけるいたずら好きの彫刻。（ドイツ・メーアスブルク）

A sculpture that periodically sprays pedestrians with water. (Meersburg, Germany)

東京・渋谷駅前広場の「ハチ公」は今でもランドマークとして親しまれ，待合場所の目印となっている。

The "Hachiko" statue in front of Shibuya Station in Tokyo is still used as a landmark for a meeting place.

昔から教会や宮殿の壁画や装飾彫刻をつくってきたオーバーアマガウの彫刻。

Oberammergau has historically made decorative sculptures and murals for churches and palaces.

ベルンではさまざまな彫刻が位置を知らせるランド
マークとして活用されている。

Various sculptures are used as landmarks in Bern
to show directions.

### 3) 地図誘導型

地図は空間の構造を把握させるために用いる。まちの中での案内地図は，簡潔で十分な情報が記載されるようにデザインする。

### Map Guidance Method

Maps are used to grasp the structure of space. Maps in cities should be designed to include concise and sufficient data.

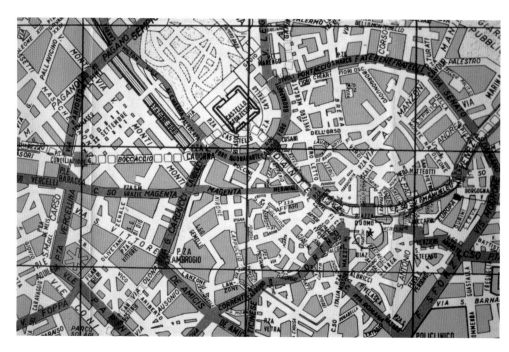

ミラノの地図。色彩のセンスとバランスがいい。

A map in Milan. The sense of color and balance are excellent.

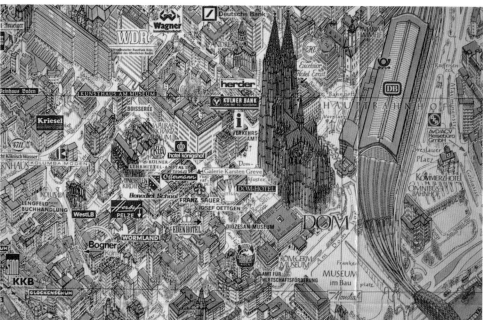

ケルンの立体地図。まちの雰囲気がよくわかる精密な作画である。現地と照合するには便利だが，頻繁に使うには煩わしい。

A cubic map in Cologne. It is an accurate display that precisely conveys the town's atmosphere. Although it is convenient to check against the actual site, it is too troublesome to use often.

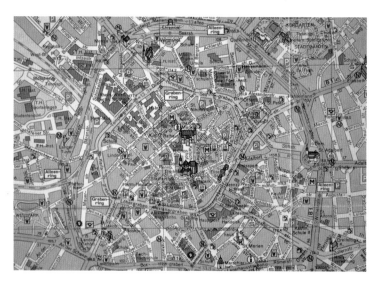

ドイツの地図。要所に強調する絵や色彩を使い，わかりやすくしている。

A German map. Pictures and colors are used to emphasize the key points.

もっともオーソドックスな地図。このまま案内サインで使うと繁雑になり，色彩もあいまいになってしまうおそれがある。

The most orthodox kind of map. It is too complex and vague in terms of color to be used as an information sign.

インターラーケンの鳥瞰地図。環境の特徴がよくわかる特殊な地図である。観光地図に徹している。

A bird's-eye view of Interlaken. This is a special map clearly expressing the environment's characteristics. It is suitable for a tourist resort.

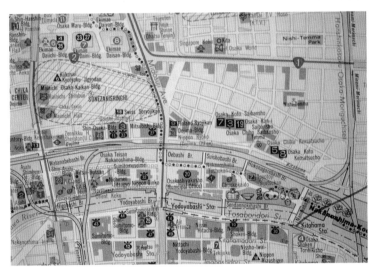

表現が改善され簡潔でわかりやすくなった。（大阪市）

The expressions were improved and are now more concise and easy to understand. (Osaka City)

ハメルンの絵地図。楽しい雰囲気が伝わってくる。大胆に単純化しているが伝えたい内容がよくわかる。

A picture map of Hameln. The gay atmosphere is conveyed well. Although boldly simplified, we can clearly understand what is being conveyed.

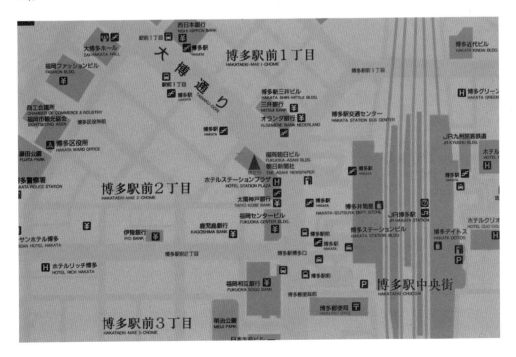

福岡市の都市サイン地図。各種の地図を分析し、都市の案内地図にふさわしい表現となっている。

A city sign map of Fukuoka City. Different kinds of maps were analyzed to select the expression most suitable for an urban information map.

# 表記することば

　最近は国際化が強調され英文が併記されることが多くなった。日本語は外国人にとってわかりにくく，英文やその他の外国語，あるいはピクトグラムを併記するのが親切である。

## 1）日本語

　サインではわかりやすく美しい日本語を表記する。独り歩きできる，小学生高学年程度の語学力で理解できることを目安とし，できるだけ平易に表現する。

## 2）外国語

　国際化に対応し，日本語を理解できない外国人でも安心して行動できるように，外国語併記を促進する。外国語は状況に応じて選択するが，一般には英語（米語）とする。表記する英文は，外国人が読めて理解できるとともに，日本人にも理解しやすいものにする。

　固有名詞は原則としてローマ字表記（ヘボン式）とする。機能を表す名詞については英語を使用し，固有の名詞であっても，日本人に普及している平易な英語については英語とする。逆に外国人が理解してしかるべき日本語については，ローマ字（ヘボン式）にするのが適当である。

## Use of Terms

　　　In response to the recent internationalization, more English terms are coming to be stated side by side together with Japanese terms. The Japanese language is hard for foreigners to understand. If English and other foreign languages or pictographs are shown together with Japanese language, that will help foreigners.

1) Japanese Languages

　　　Easy-to-understand and pleasant terms should be used for signs. They should be easily understood even by primary school children in higher grades, and the easiest possible terms should be used.

2) Foreign Languages

　　　It is urged that going with internationalization, foreign languages also should be written side by side together with Japanese terms, so as to help foreigners understand what is stated, and help them move toward their destinations will no fear. Which foreign language should be used will be decided, depending upon circumstances. Generally speaking, English(American English) is used. Statement in English should be such as to be read and understood by non-English speaking foreigners and also by Japanese people.

　　　In principle, the Roman alphabet (Hepburn) should be used for proper nouns. For nouns indicating functions, English should be used. For English proper nouns which have so widely spread among Japanese people as to be understood by them, English should be used. Likewise, it is better to state in the Roman alphabet the words which foreigners can understand.

独創的な形をした公園のサイン。注意を促すよう形を工夫している。

A uniquely shaped sign in a park. The shape is creative and attracts the attention of people.

公共のサインでは，表記する情報をその目的や意味によって明確に整理する。情報過多だったり，少なすぎる場合も逆効果になる場合があるので注意する。現在使われている日本語を簡潔に，美しいデザインで表現する。

It is necessary to clearly organize the purpose and meaning of the data conveyed when designing public signs. Only a negative effect will be achieved if there is too much or too little data included. The currently used Japanese should be expressed concisely, with an attractive design.

工夫されたゴミの取り扱い案内。

A creative information sign for handing waste.

国際化が進む中、英文併記が一般化してきた。

Japan becomes more international, it is now popular to include English on signs.

## 凡例     Index

**福岡市公共施設**
Public Facilities of Fukuoka City
Equipement Municipal
福冈市公共设施
후쿠오카시공공시설

**インフォメーション**
Information
Renseignements
讯问处
인포메이션

**観光お勧め地点**
Points of Interest
Site Touristique
重要观光点
관광지

**JR駅**
JR Station
Gare JR
JR站
JR역

**西鉄駅**
NISHITETSU Station
Gare NISHITETSU
西铁站
니시테츠역

**地下鉄駅**
Subway
Metro
地铁站
지하철역

**バスセンター，バス停**
Bus Stop
Gare routiere, Arrèt d autobus
公共汽车中心，公共汽车站
버스센타, 버스 정류장

**タクシー乗場**
Taxi Stop
Station de taxi
出租汽车乗车场
택시

**乗船場**
Warf
Embarcadere
乗船马头
승선장

**美術館，博物館**
Museum
Musee
美术馆，博物馆
미술관, 박물관

**ホール**
Concert Hall
Salle de spectacle
大厅
호올

**神社**
Shrine
Temple shintoiste
神社
신사

**寺院**
Temple
Temple(bouddhique)
寺院
사찰

**駐車場**
Parking Lot
Parc de stationnement
停车场
주차장

**郵便局**
Post Office
Poste
邮局
우체국

**銀行**
Bank
Banque
银行
은행

**大規模商業施設**
Shopping Center
Centre commercial
大型商业区
백화점, 시장

**ホテル，旅館**
Hotel, Inn
Hôtel
饭店, 旅馆
호텔, 여관

**NTT**

**警察署，派出所**
Police
Police
**警察署，派出所**
警察署, 派出所
경찰서, 파출소

**病院**
Hospital
Hôpital
医院
병원

**学校**
School
Ecole
学校
학교

**図書館**
Library
Bibliotheque
图书馆
도서관

福岡市では，英文のほかフランス語，中国語，韓国語（ハングル）を併記し，国際都市のイメージづくりをしている。

Fukuoka City has begun using English, French, Chinese, and Korean on their signs, creating an international image.

身振り手振り，会話，手紙や電話，ビデオやコンピュータによる通信など，コミュニケーションのための表現手段が著しく多様化してきた。サインにおいても普通は文字やピクトグラム（絵文字），図や写真などによって表記するが，最新の映像媒体を活用したものや自然の景観を利用したものも珍しくない。既成概念や新・珍・奇といった概念にとらわれることなく，伝達しようとする内容や目的に適った表現方法を選択する。

### 1）文字

文字は物事を普遍的に分析的に伝えることができる。そのため記名や内容の説明，注意・禁止などの表現に向いている。ただし屋外ではその内容を読み取る集中力が長続きしないので，無理なく読み取る文字量は，およそ200文字，30秒程度が限界とされている。視点が1点にとどまるおよそ0.3秒では約15文字しか読めない計算になる。こうした人間の視覚的な目安を考えて情報を整理すると理解されやすくなる。

文字の書体にはいろいろな種類があるが，ゴシック体や明朝体が一般に使われている。その他毛筆文字，手書き文字，さまざまな創作文字が発表されている。読みやすさやデザインとの調和を考えて書体を選択する。最近は英文を併記することも多く，アルファベットとの調和も考えてデザインするとよい。

### 2）ピクトグラム（絵記号）

ピクトグラムは，伝えたい情報を象徴化し簡潔でわかりやすく表現する。わかりにくい内容を要約し，遠くから見ても視認でき，瞬間的に意味を伝え，また文字が読めない人や外国人にもその内容が伝えられる役割をもっている。

基本的な行動にかかわるものや，防災上の意味を伝えるピクトグラムについては国際的に共通化しようとする動きがあり，特定の機関で定めたピクトグラムもある。その他，国際空港などの交通機関では，アメリカ運輸省が提案したピクトグラムが普及しつつある。

共通化するものと独自性を強調するものについては，その都度適正な判断を下すべきで，画一化を避け独自のピクトグラムを作ることが多いが，暗号化しかえってわかりにくくなるおそれもあるので，注意したい。

### 3）図・写真

図にはイラストレーション，写真，グラフ，地図などの形態がある。視覚的に解説を補い，ダイレクトな理解を促す。

イラストレーションや写真は，その場で直接見ることのできない情報（地球の内部構造，昔の生活の様子，飛んでいる鳥，星座など）をわかりやすく説明するときなどに有効である。

グラフは，交通機関の時刻や，都市の人口の変遷など動態的な推移と時間と空間の変化を伝える内容の伝達に適している。

地図は空間の構成を把握するために用いられる。設置する場所が適切であれば大きな安心感が与えられる。地図には地形を表す地形図や地下鉄などの路線を表す特殊図などさまざまな形がある。その表現方法も具象的なものから抽象的なものまで多様である。

### 4）映像媒体

映像による情報伝達は，最近急速に注目されている。主要な駅や交通拠点でも観光のポイントを直ちに検索できるようにしたデータベースが普及し，マルチビジョンや大型ビジョンなども目につくようになっている。従来の観光案内の内容をそのままニューメディアに置き換えてもあまり意味がないと思うが，新しい発想での活用を考えればかなり有効なメディアの活用となるであろう。

コンピュータの発達と連動する通信ネットワークや光レーザーディスクなどの普及によって，ハイビジョンの実用化やデータベースの映像化の動きもあり，現に岐阜県の美術館では所蔵している美術品の映像入力化が行われ，今後の展示方法に新しい時代の到来を告げている。フランスのポンピドーセンターも，この方式に関心を寄せており，映像は説得力のある情報伝達の技法として，今後の研究課題として注目しておかねばならぬ動きである。

JRのサイン。左は古いタイプで 右は 新しいタイプ。サインの書体は機能が要求されるところでは感性よりも明確さが要求される。そのうえ読みやすく美しいことが基本である。

JR signs. Old type. New type.
When function is sought in the character type of a sign, it is important to stress accuracy rather than sensitivity. The characters must also be attractive and easy to read.

交通標識では，文字の瞬間的な可読性が要求される。情報量が多いにもかかわらず，表現上の約束事を明確に定めて，わかりやすくしてある。

Words and characters on traffic signs must be instantly understood. Although the amount of data is great, clear standards of expression have been set, so that the information is easily understood.

## Means Used for Expressions

The means of representation are becoming markedly diversified. Gestures, conversations, letters, telephones, video-tapes, and computers are being used for the establishment of communications. Letters, picture symbols (pictogram), charts and photographs have been used as signs, but signs using images, scenes from nature, etc., are now seen very often. For the transmission of ideas and purposes, the most appropriate way of presenting them should be chosen from among those which will meet the purpose, not to be bound by already-existing ideas and free from desires to seek novelty and eccentricity.

### 1) Letters

Ideas can be transmitted universally and analytically by the use of letters, which are a proper means to show names, explain contents, give caution, place a ban, etc. When one is outside buildings, he cannot concentrate himself long enough to read lengthy statements. The number of words should be limited to about 200, which he can read to the last in about 30 seconds. It is calculated that one can read 15 characters in 0.3 second. Information that is drawn up, by taking these characteristics about man's visual power into account, will be easy to understand.

There are various types of characters, the most popular of which are the boldface and Ming types. There is also writing by "fude(brush)," hand-writing, and unique characteristic writings. For signs, styles that can be read with no difficulty should be used. Recently English terms are often stated together with Japanese words. When signs are designed, while keeping in mind harmony with English terms, they will produce good effects.

### 2) Pictogram

Pictogram is a means to symbolize the contents of information in an easy-to-understand and concise form. Pictogram can be seen from a distance, and even illiterates and foreigners can easily understand what is symbolized.

Movements have started calling for establishing international standards for pictographs for the prevention of disasters, the promotion of basic human moves, etc. Some organs have formulated standards for pictogram. The pictogram proposed by the US Department of Transportation is coming to be used widely at international airports and other transportation facilities.

Proper judgment should be formed on whether common sense or individuality should be stressed in drawing up pictographs. There are many cases where creativeness is valued too greatly, even at the cost of clearness. If they are made too original, they may become something like codes and it will become hard to understand. This should be avoided.

### 3) Visual Matters and Photographs

For visual matters, there are such forms as illustrations, photographs, graphs, maps, etc. They promote viewers' understanding directly by visually supplementing comments.

Illustrations and photographs are effective in explaining in a simple way information on things which cannot be seen on the spot (the inner structure of the earth; the ancient mode of living; birds flying; constellations; etc.)

Graphs are suitable for transmitting information on statistical changes, such as changes in urban population, time and space.

Maps are used to help grasp the formation of space. If they are put up in proper places, they will have viewers feel assured. There are varieties of forms for maps from topographical maps to special maps for subway routes, etc. The design of some maps is concrete while that of some other maps is abstract. Maps are illustrated in various ways.

### 4) Images

The transmission of information by image is quickly attracting attention. At big stations and transportation keypoints, data bases have been installed, aiming to help tourists look for the sight-seeing spots they will visit. Quite many multi-visions and large-size visions are now seen in various places. The mere change of the form from ordinary sight-seeing guidance to new media will not be so significant. However, if new media using images are drawn up based on a new concept, that will be of great help.

The spread of communications networks and optical laser disks was brought about by the development of computers. Now moves have started calling for the practical use of high-vision images and the use of images for data bases. The Gifu Prefectural Art Museum has completed preparations for presenting the images of the paintings it has collected on the screen. The Museum has become a forerunner of the age of new exhibitions. The Pompidou Center of France is showing strong interest in this formula. The use of images is an information transmission technique with strong persuasive power. This move must be noted with attention as a subject matter for study in the future.

文字の大きさと判読距離
LETTER SIZE AND READABLE DISTANCE

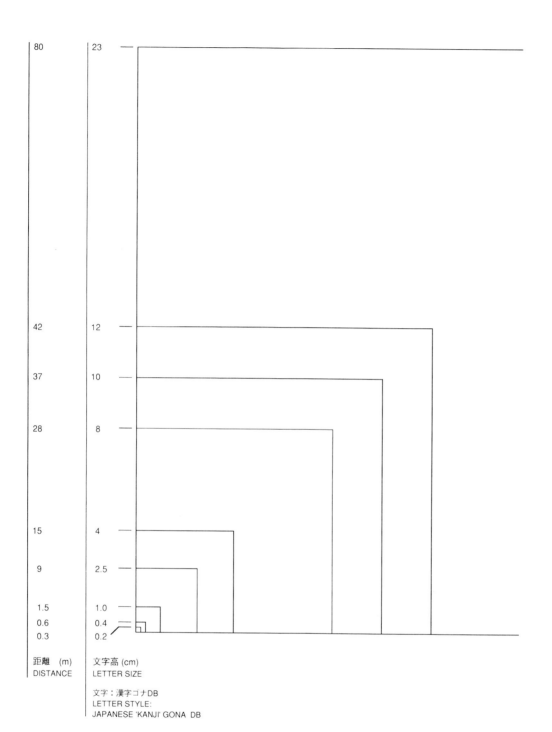

| 80 | 23 |
| 42 | 12 |
| 37 | 10 |
| 28 | 8 |
| 15 | 4 |
| 9 | 2.5 |
| 1.5 | 1.0 |
| 0.6 | 0.4 |
| 0.3 | 0.2 |

距離 (m)
DISTANCE

文字高 (cm)
LETTER SIZE

文字：漢字ゴナDB
LETTER STYLE:
JAPANESE 'KANJI' GONA DB

文字の大きさと判読距離の関係。文字の大きさをど
れくらいにするかは，読みやすさと美しさ，景観へ
の配慮も考えてデザインしなくてはならない。表は
文字の大きさとそれが見える距離の関係をまとめた
もの。一応の目安でありいろいろな条件によって変
わってくる。

The relationship between the size and distance of
characters. When determining the size of character. it is also necessary to consider the legibility
and beauty of character, as well as the surrounding scenery. The table shows the relationship
between the size of character and distance from
which they were legible. These are only general
standards. and should be altered according to a
variety of conditions.

## 書体の瞬間的な読みやすさ
## FAST READBLE LETTER STYLE

| 書体<br>LETTER STYLE | 図<br>FIGURE | 刺激例<br>SAMPLE | 可読文字数（5文字中）<br>READING CAPACITY<br>(PER 5 LETTER UNIT)<br>提示時間 DISPLAY TIME (SEC.)<br>0.01 | <br><br><br>0.3 |
|---|---|---|---|---|
| 細明朝体<br>MINCHO LIGHT | ポジ<br>POSITIVE | 宰木府鳥甘 | 1.4 | 3.3 |
| | ネガ<br>NEGATIVE | 宰木府鳥甘 | 2.3 | 3.5 |
| 中明朝体<br>MINCHO REGULAR | ポジ<br>POSITIVE | 野二木佐鳥 | 2.0 | 3.2 |
| | ネガ<br>NEGATIVE | 野二木佐鳥 | 2.3 | 3.2 |
| 太明朝体<br>MINCHO BOLD | ポジ<br>POSITIVE | 紫野宰甘太 | 1.6 | 3.5 |
| | ネガ<br>NEGATIVE | 紫野宰甘太 | 2.1 | 3.6 |
| ゴナM<br>GONA M | ポジ<br>POSITIVE | 留福二栖佐 | 1.9 | 2.7 |
| | ネガ<br>NEGATIVE | 留福二栖佐 | 2.7 | 3.5 |
| ゴナDB<br>GONA DB | ポジ<br>POSITIVE | 府宰木栖紫 | 2.0 | 3.2 |
| | ネガ<br>NEGATIVE | 府宰木栖紫 | 2.6 | 3.0 |
| ナールL<br>NAR L | ポジ<br>POSITIVE | 紫鳥米二宰 | 2.1 | 3.1 |
| | ネガ<br>NEGATIVE | 紫鳥米二宰 | 2.4 | 3.3 |
| ナールD<br>NAR D | ポジ<br>POSITIVE | 木宰鳥米賀 | 2.0 | 3.5 |
| | ネガ<br>NEGATIVE | 木宰鳥米賀 | 2.3 | 3.4 |
| ナールE<br>NAR E | ポジ<br>POSITIVE | 鳥宰久太紫 | 2.2 | 3.4 |
| | ネガ<br>NEGATIVE | 鳥宰久太紫 | 2.4 | 3.2 |

文字の可読性についての調査。書体の瞬間的な読みやすさを調べたもの。1文字の大きさは10cm，被験者との距離は3m。書体別の数字は5文字を提示し，判読できた文字数は表のとおりである。短い時間ではゴナ（角ゴシック）とナール（丸ゴシック）の中太が読みやすいことがわかった。

A survey on the legibility of writing. The instant comprehension of different styles of writing has been researched. Each character's size is 10cm, and was placed 3m from the subject. Five numbers of different styles were shown. The legible characters have been listed here. It was found that the easily comprehensible characters were the square and round Gothic letters of medium thickness.

伝統的な文字をうまく使った例。

An example in which traditional characters are used cleverly.

日本は象形文字や漢字を使う文化圏であるため，看板に文字を使用する例が多い。用途や目的に応じて書体を決めたりロゴタイプを特別にデザインする。

Since Japan is in the cultural area using hieroglyphs and Chinese characters, many signs are designed using writing. The character style should be chosen according to the usage and purpose, in some cases designing special logotypes.

新旧さまざまな書体。

Old and new types of character styles.

1）ピクトグラムを決めるときは，言語の代わりをする
　　こと。
2）国際的な共通性があること。
3）土地不案内な人にも理解できること。
4）設置現場での照らし合わせができるようになってい
　　ること。
5）対象とする種類や特徴が認識されるものてあること。
6）その国や外国の言語が意味するものを補うこと。
　　などの条件をふまえて制作する。
　　福岡市と佐賀市はこういう条件を設定した上でピク
　トグラムを策定している。(アメリカの運輸省が制定
　しているピクトグラムをリ・デザインしたものを含
　む。)

The following are the conditions for designing
pictograms:
1) The pictograms must be used as a substitute for
   language.
2) There must be an internationally recognizable
   commonness.
3) People not accustomed to the area must be able
   to understand them.
4) It must be possible to check and compare the
   information at the actual site.
5) The particular type and characteristics that are
   the object must be recognizable.
6) They must supplement the language or meaning
   of the country's language.
   The cities of Fukuoke and Saga plan pictograms
   according to these standards. (The pictograms
   from the U.S. Ministry of Transport that have
   been re-designed are included.)

インフォメーション
INFORMATION

空港
AIRPORT PORT

観光お勧め地点
ATTRACTION POINT

JR駅
JR STATION

乗船場
WARF

海水浴場,プール
SWIMING

バスセンター,バス停
BUS CENTER,STOP

タクシー乗り場
TAXI STAND

ホテル,旅館
HOTEL,INN

警察
POLICE

病院
HOSPITAL

レストラン
RESTAURANT

学校
SCHOOL

郵便局
POST OFFICE

駐車場
PARKING

銀行
BANK

NTT
NTT

駐輪場,サイクリング道路
BICYCLE LOT,CYCLING ROAD

美術館,博物館
MUSEUM

図書館
LIBRARY

外国施設
INTERNATIONAL FACILITIES

神社 SHRINE
 寺院 TEMPLE
 教会 CHURCH
 大規模商業施設 SHOPPING AREA
 切符売り場,受付 TICKET,RECEPTION

 ヨットハーバー YACHT HARBOR
 キャンプ場 CAMPING GROUND
 水飲み WATER TO DRINK
 WC WC
 身体障害者用施設 HANDICAPPED

 コンサートホール CONCERT HALL
 映画館 MOVIE THEATER
 コインロッカー COIN LOCKER
 男 GENTLEMEN
 女 LADIES

 コーヒーショップ COFFEE SHOP
 売店（軽食） SNACK BAR
 売店 KIOSK
 エレベーター ELEVATOR
 エスカレーター ESCALATOR

 駐車禁止 NO PARKING
 喫煙(所) SMOKING（ROOM）
 禁煙 NO SMOKING
 階段 STAIRS
 非常口 EMERGENCY EXIT

 駐輪禁止 NO PARKING
 ロビー LOBBY
 会議室 CONFERENCE ROOM
 立ち入り禁止 NO ADMITTANCE
 工事中 UNDER CONSTRUCTION

 国際電話 INTERNATIONAL TELEPHONE
 電話 TELEPHONE
 まいご LOST CHILD
 矢印 ARROW

別表）
地図に使われているピクトグラム。地図の用途によっては対象と表現が異なる。

Table
Pictograms used on maps. The object and expression are different according to the map's usage.

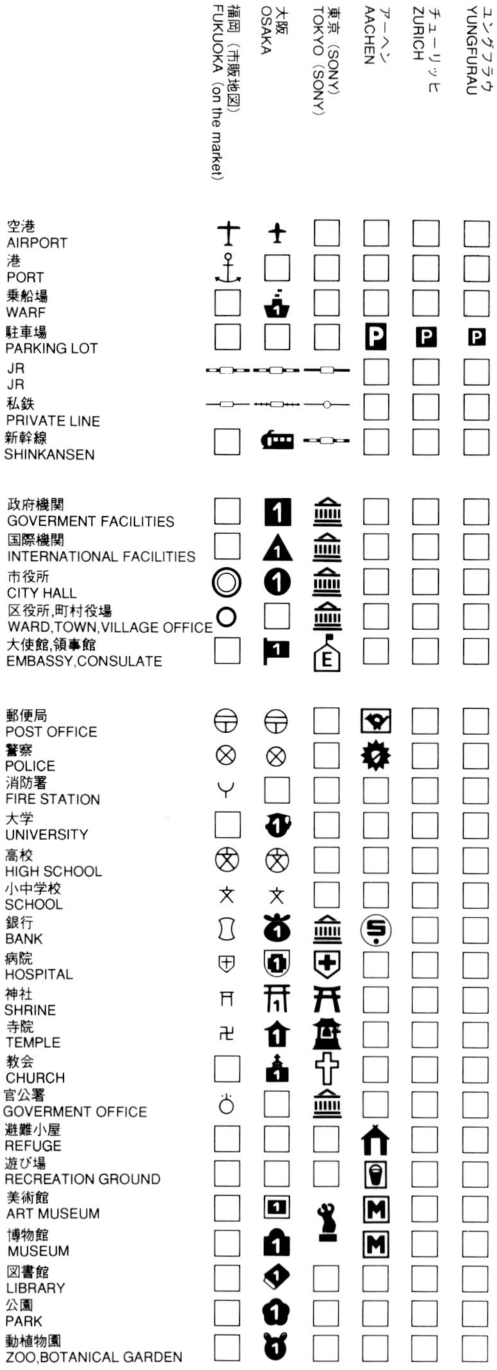

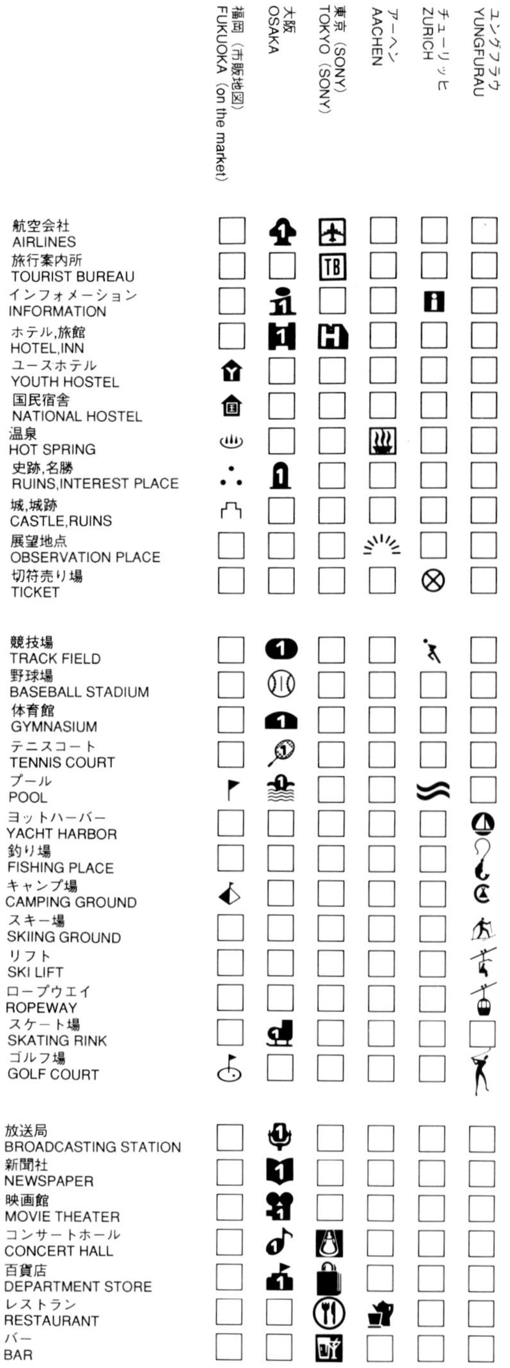

Column headers (both halves):
福岡（市販地図）FUKUOKA (on the market) / 大阪 OSAKA / 東京 (SONY) TOKYO (SONY) / アーヘン AACHEN / チューリッヒ ZURICH / ユングフラウ YUNGFURAU

Left half rows:

| | 福岡 FUKUOKA | 大阪 OSAKA | 東京 TOKYO (SONY) | アーヘン AACHEN | チューリッヒ ZURICH | ユングフラウ YUNGFURAU |
|---|---|---|---|---|---|---|
| 空港 AIRPORT | | ✝ | ✝ | | | |
| 港 PORT | | ⚓ | | | | |
| 乗船場 WARF | | 🚢 | | | | |
| 駐車場 PARKING LOT | | | | P | P | P |
| JR | | ─○─ | | | | |
| 私鉄 PRIVATE LINE | | ─○─ | | | | |
| 新幹線 SHINKANSEN | | 🚈 | | | | |
| 政府機関 GOVERMENT FACILITIES | | 1 | 血 | | | |
| 国際機関 INTERNATIONAL FACILITIES | | ▲ | 血 | | | |
| 市役所 CITY HALL | ◎ | 1 | 血 | | | |
| 区役所,町村役場 WARD,TOWN,VILLAGE OFFICE | ○ | | 血 | | | |
| 大使館,領事館 EMBASSY,CONSULATE | | 🏴 1 | Ⓔ | | | |
| 郵便局 POST OFFICE | ⊖ | ⊖ | | ✹ | | |
| 警察 POLICE | ⊗ | ⊗ | | ✸ | | |
| 消防署 FIRE STATION | Y | | | | | |
| 大学 UNIVERSITY | | 1 | | | | |
| 高校 HIGH SCHOOL | ⊗ | ⊗ | | | | |
| 小中学校 SCHOOL | ✕ | ✕ | | | | |
| 銀行 BANK | | 8 | 血 | Ⓢ | | |
| 病院 HOSPITAL | 田 | 1 | ✚ | | | |
| 神社 SHRINE | 卅 | 卅 | 卅 | | | |
| 寺院 TEMPLE | 卍 | 1 | | | | |
| 教会 CHURCH | | 1 | ✝ | | | |
| 官公署 GOVERMENT OFFICE | ○ | | 血 | | | |
| 避難小屋 REFUGE | | | | 🏠 | | |
| 遊び場 RECREATION GROUND | | | | 🎈 | | |
| 美術館 ART MUSEUM | | 1 | | M | | |
| 博物館 MUSEUM | | 1 | | M | | |
| 図書館 LIBRARY | | ◆ | | | | |
| 公園 PARK | | 1 | | | | |
| 動植物園 ZOO,BOTANICAL GARDEN | | 8 | | | | |

Right half rows:

| | 福岡 FUKUOKA | 大阪 OSAKA | 東京 TOKYO (SONY) | アーヘン AACHEN | チューリッヒ ZURICH | ユングフラウ YUNGFURAU |
|---|---|---|---|---|---|---|
| 航空会社 AIRLINES | | ✈ | ✈ | | | |
| 旅行案内所 TOURIST BUREAU | | | TB | | | |
| インフォメーション INFORMATION | | i | | | i | |
| ホテル,旅館 HOTEL,INN | | 1 | H | | | |
| ユースホテル YOUTH HOSTEL | ⛺ | | | | | |
| 国民宿舎 NATIONAL HOSTEL | 🏠 | | | | | |
| 温泉 HOT SPRING | ♨ | | | ♨ | | |
| 史跡,名勝 RUINS,INTEREST PLACE | ∴ | 1 | | | | |
| 城,城跡 CASTLE,RUINS | 🏰 | | | | | |
| 展望地点 OBSERVATION PLACE | | | | ☀ | | |
| 切符売り場 TICKET | | | | | ⊗ | |
| 競技場 TRACK FIELD | | 1 | | 🏃 | | |
| 野球場 BASEBALL STADIUM | | ⚾ | | | | |
| 体育館 GYMNASIUM | | 1 | | | | |
| テニスコート TENNIS COURT | | 🎾 | | | | |
| プール POOL | 🚩 | ≋ | | | ≋ | |
| ヨットハーバー YACHT HARBOR | | | | | | ⛵ |
| 釣り場 FISHING PLACE | | | | | | 🎣 |
| キャンプ場 CAMPING GROUND | ◆ | | | | | 🏕 |
| スキー場 SKIING GROUND | | | | | | ⛷ |
| リフト SKI LIFT | | | | | | 🚡 |
| ロープウエイ ROPEWAY | | | | | | 🚠 |
| スケート場 SKATING RINK | | ⛸ | | | | |
| ゴルフ場 GOLF COURT | ⛳ | | | | | ⛳ |
| 放送局 BROADCASTING STATION | | 🎤 | | | | |
| 新聞社 NEWSPAPER | | 1 | | | | |
| 映画館 MOVIE THEATER | | 🎬 | | | | |
| コンサートホール CONCERT HALL | | ♪ | 🔔 | | | |
| 百貨店 DEPARTMENT STORE | | 1 | 🛍 | | | |
| レストラン RESTAURANT | | 🍴 | 🍴 | | 🍴 | |
| バー BAR | | 🍸 | | | | |

96

韓国ソウルの地下鉄のサイン。ピクトグラムを使っ
ているので外国人にも理解でき安心感を与えている。

A sign for the Seoul subway system in Korea.
Pictograms are used, so even foreigners can
understand the signs and feel safe.

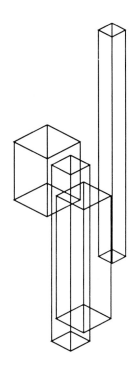

# 3.サインの素材と形

Materials and Styles of Designs

サインを製作する上で代表的な素材について触れておきたい。サインの素材は数多いが，その代表的なものには次のようなものがある。

**1）石材**

古くから建物や彫刻の材料として使われてきた。経年変化が少なく安定した素材である。重量感があり，加工機械や技術の発展によって，加工度が進んでいる。今までは文字を刻むなどの簡単な表示素材として使われることが多かったが，表面仕上げの方法や彫刻物としての加工度合と石材の接着剤の進歩によって，かなり重量のあるものも使えるようになって，2～30トンある素材を分割して加工することもでき，他の材料との組み合わせを考えれば，多彩な表現が可能になっている。

**2）木材**

天然の風合いには捨て難いものがある。適当に風化することを逆手にとった景観にマッチする素材として，最近注目を浴びている。防腐材の使用，防腐加工の技術の開発で，屋外で使用しても，かなりの年数もつようになった。表示素材としても古くから使われており，着色なども工夫すれば，素朴な味と人間にやさしい趣を引き出すことができる。使い方によってはモダンになったり，高級感を出すことができる。

**3）鋳物**

鉄やアルミニュウムの鋳物は，比較的自由な型に成型できる素材で，比較的少量の生産も可能である。構造強度や精密性はやや劣るが，経年変化が少なく，落ち着きが感じられ親しみやすい。かなり自由な着色も可能だが，素材の質感を損なわぬ程度にとどめたい。文字もゴシックの漢字で8mm程度まで読み取れる。鋳物は加工技術の進歩によって表示素材として将来性がある。

**4）アルミ押し出し成型**

アルミは押し出し成型によって自由な断面形状が得られ，独創的なデザインを強調できる。大量生産でコストダウンできるが，少量の場合は高価になる。

**5）鋼管**

ステンレス・スチール，一般鋼管など各種ある。比較的軽量簡便でサインには多く使われてきた。一般的にポール型サインに使いやすい。素材のままでは単調になり

やすいので，デザインを工夫する必要がある。鉄は錆やすく入念な維持管理と点検を考えた構造にしておくべきであろう。

**6）鋼材**

屋外で長期的に風雨にさらされるものには，ステンレス・スチールやアルミがよく使われる。一般鋼材は防錆処理が必要で，樹脂をサンドイッチして軽量化した新素材もある。鋼材は一般に人工的で冷たい印象がある反面，都会的で洗練されたイメージがある。表示はスクリーン印刷が一般的だが，屋外では褪色しやすい。ステンレス・スチールやアルミのエッチングは高級感があり耐久性も高い。アルミ写真板は仕上がりの精度が高いが，品質管理が難しく，屋外での耐久性はスクリーン印刷と大差ない。

**7）ガラス強化セメント**

コンクリートと樹脂の中間的な素材で街路の小工作物によく使われる。コンクリートより微細な表現ができ強度もある。しかし，年月の経過とともに脆くなり表面から劣化が進み破損しやすくなるようである。

**8）コンクリート**

比較的廉価で安定した供給が得られるため，今まで非常に多く使われてきた。任意の造形が可能で，流し込みの型も芸術的なものまで開発されている。しかし汚れや変色などが防ぎにくく，どのようなデザインを施すかが課題である。

**9）ガラス**

割れやすいイメージがあるが，縁取りに工夫すればかなりの強度が得られ，パリのバス停などでは道路に面した部分にもかなり広い面積で使われており，開放感がある。サインでは表示部分を保護するために使われ，単独で使用されることは少ないが，サンドブラストやエッチングなどのデザインによってガラスならではの芸術性を引き出すことも可能である。

またステンドグラスも今後使用されることが多くなると思われ，素材としてのおもしろみが期待できる。

**10）樹脂**

一般的によく使われている素材である。安価で加工しやすいが，表面強度が低く傷がつきやすい。年月とともに割れやすくなる。ガラスとは違った独特の風合いを活用するデザインにすれば，いろいろなところで使える素材である。最近はポリカーボネートなどの強度の高い素材が開発されていて，表示素材として使われる機会が増えている。

**11）陶板**

建築の外装材などによく使われるようになった。経年変化がすくなく，天然素材ならではの風合いがあるが，屋外での使用には剝離したり壊れたりしないように接着面や角部分の処理をに工夫をする必要がある。表示素材として最近急速に使われており，正確なデザインと自由な色彩が使える利点がある。床面に使う場合，雨天のときのスリップを防ぐ配慮が必要であろう。

**12）シート材**

高輝度反射シートは自動車向けのサインで使用されており，ヘッドライトの光で反射し，文字などを明瞭に視認できる。一般にアルミ板に熱圧着させて使用する。

カッティングシートなどの一般シート材は店舗の看板や内装ディスプレイによく使われている。色数も豊富で加工しやすいところから，カラフルな塗装に代わって使われる事例が増えている。

素材にあまり手を加えず構成した石のモニュメント。 The material was left relatively untouched to construct this stone monument.

地方都市の典型的なインフォメーション。

Typical information of a suburban city.

I would like to take up materials used for designing signs. The following are typical materials:

1) Stone

Stone has been used since old times as a material for buildings and sculptures. The processing of massive and heavy stone has seen great progress due to the development of processing machines and techniques. Stone was mostly used in the past by using simple techniques, engraving letters on its surface, etc. However, due to progress of processing techniques and adhesive agents, such as the technique of finishing the surface of stone, it has become possible to the quite heavy stone weighing two to thirty tons as a material for sculptures, etc. If stone is used in combination with other materials, diversified designing will become possible.

2) Wood

The natural touch of wood is appealing. It is now noted as an attractive material which goes with natural scenery, especially when it has become weathered. After the development of antiseptic agents and processing techniques, wood products are able to stand against weathers for a considerably long time, even when they are placed outdoors. Wood has been used as a material for showing the names of persons, places, etc. If various devices are made, by painting wood, etc., a simple taste and a feeling warm to man will be drawn out of it. Depending on how it is used, it will look modern and will have a high-quality atmosphere.

3) Cast Metals

Iron and aluminum are cast metals which can be comparatively freely modeled. The production of a limited number of works is possible. Although their structural strength and precision degree leave something to be desired, they do not undergo changes for many years. They have a quiet atmosphere and viewers will feel closeness toward these materials. Considerably many colors can be used for them, but colors should be used within the limit of not spoiling their quality as cast metals. It is possible to read up to about 8mm Gothic type Chinese characters imprited on them. When cast metal processing techniques make progress, they will become promising materials.

4) Aluminum Press Type

Aluminum can be pressed freely and varieties of section forms are obtained. It is possible to stress originality in designs. Costs can be reduced by mass production. When a small amount is produced, costs will become higher.

5) Steel Tube

Several kinds of steel tube are available, including stainless steel and general steel tube. This comparatively light-weight and handy-to-use material has been widely used for signs. It is generally used for ball-type signs. Stainless steel as a material is somewhat monotonous, and therefore, ingenuity should be displayed in designs. When iron is used, which easily gets rusty, its structure should be designed, while taking into account how to maintain and control it, and how to carry out a check.

6) Steel Materials

Stainless steel and aluminum are often used when signs are placed in a place where they are exposed to rain and wind for a long period of time. Anti-corrosive treatment is necessary for ordinary steel materials. A new light-weight steel material which is sandwitched in between resin coating is also available. Steel materials generally give an artificial and cool impression, but on the other hand, there is an urban and refined atmosphere about them. Screen printing is generally used for designing these materials. When steel material-used signs are placed outdoors painted colors tend to fade away soon. There is a high-grade atmosphere about stainless steel and aluminum etching, and it also has durability. The finishing of aluminum photo plate is highly precise, but it is difficult to maintain its quality. Its durability when placed outdoors is almost the same as that of screen printing.

7) Glass-Tempered Cement

This is a material which is something like being in between concrete and resin, and is often used for small-size signs put up on the street. When this material is used, it is possible to make more minute designs than when concrete is used. This material is also strong. It seems, however, that with the pass of time its surface becomes easily breakable.

8) Concrete

The supply of concrete is stable and it can be obtained comparably at low prices. This is why it has so far been used very extensively. It can be freely molded into any forms. Artistic molds have also been developed. However, it is difficult to prevent it from becoming stained and its colors becoming faded. As a task for the future, it is necessary to study what designs are suitable for this material.

9) Glass

Glass gives the impression that it easily gets cracked. However, if its edge is processed properly, its intensity will increase. At some bus stops in Paris, glass panels are set up facing sidewalks. This gives a sense of openness. Glass is used to protect symbols on signs. It is scarecely used by itself. When sandblast or etching is used for designing glass, that will create an artistic feeling special to glass.

Stained glass will probably by used more frequently than before. It is expected that it will become an attractive material from now on.

10) Resin

Resin is widely used because its prices are low and it can be processed easily. However, its surface is not so strong and with the progress of time, it cracks easily. If designs are made utilizing this material's unique feeling which is quite different from glass, resin can be used in many ways. recently polycarbonate with strong intensity has been developed. Resin is being used on increasingly many occasions.

11) Ceramic Tiles

They are now widely used as a building exterior material. They seldom sustain changes, even used for many years, and have a feeling which is special only to natural materials. However, when they are used outside buildings, it is necessary to use adhesive agents and to give special treatment as to corner parts, so that they will not peel off or break while being used for many years. Their use as a material for signs has been quickly increasing. Ceramic tiles are good, in that accurate designing becomes possible when they are used, and that any colors can be freely used. in case these tiles are used for outdoor flooring, it is necessary to use contrivances for the prevention of slip.

12) Sheet Materials

The highly shinning reflection sheet is used as signs to help automobile drivers. It reflects at automobile headlights, and helps drivers read clearly what is written. Generally, the sheet is pressed with heat on aluminum plates.

General sheet materials, such as a cutting sheet, are mostly used for store signboards and interior displays. They are now increasingly used in place of colorful painting because a large number of colors can be used for sheet materials, and also they can be processed easily.

河畔の整備にあたって地元に伝わるカッパの伝説を
生かした彫刻。

While equipping the riverside, a sculpture was
made based on the local "kappa" (water imp)
legend.

日本にも古くから伝わっている石の方向案内。(福岡
県篠栗町)

A traditional Japanese direction sign made of
stone. (Sasagiri-machi, Fukuoka Prefecture)

円柱に文字を彫刻したサイン。文字の扱いがうまい。
(チューリッヒ)

Characters have been engraved into a column to
create this sign. The characters have been
handled well. (Zurich)

木がもつ素朴な味を生かした，アジア太平洋博覧会のランドマーク。（1989年，福岡市）

The landmark of the Asia Pacific Exposition takes advantage of the natural, simple characteristics of wood. (Fukuoka City, 1989)

木の看板は昔からよく使われてきた。環境にもなじみやすく，親しみやすい。（メーアスブルク）

Wooden signs have historically been used. They blend in with the environment well, and easily become familiar to the people. (Meersburg)

木製の標識を採用するときは，汚れと劣化を考慮したうえでデザインする必要がある。

When using wooden signs, it is important to design them taking into consideration dirt and deterioration.

加工や彩色が容易で細かい表現ができる。オーナーの品性やすぐれた感性が伝わってくる。

Processing and coloring are easy, and minute expressions are possible. The owner's refinement and sensitivity are conveyed.

伝統的な景観を配慮した木の標識。

A wooden sign taking into consideration the traditional scenery.

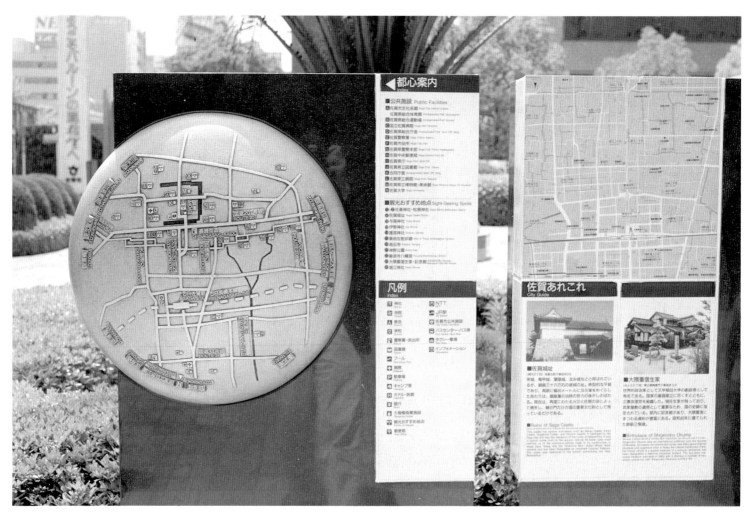

鋳物は耐久性があり，自由な形がつくれる可塑性が
ある。触りたくなる半円球の地図。

Cast metal is durable, and its plasticity enables
easy shaping. We feel the urge to touch this semi-
circular sphere map.

鋳物の特徴を生かしたサイン

A sign taking advantage of the characteristics of
cast metal.

アルミ押出成型型材のフレーム。高価だが独特なデ
ザインができる。

A pressed aluminum frame. Although costly, the
material is suited for unique designs.

ポール型のサインにもステンレスが使われるように
なった。

Stainless steel is often used now for pole-type
signs, as well.

ステンレスは耐久性にすぐれ都会的な味を引き出せ
るが，ときにはクールな印象を与えやすい。

Although stainless steel is durable and suited for
conveying an urban air, it sometimes gives a cold
impression.

金属の持ち味を生かしたサイン。（東京都庁）

A sign taking advantage of the characteristics of
metal. (Tokyo Metropolitan Government Office)

ステンレスのエッチング・サイン。高級なイメージ
が出せる。

A stainless steel, etched sign. A high class image
is achieved.

樹脂にクロマリン印刷した解説サイン。裏面に印刷して耐久性を向上させている。

An explanation sign made of resin with croma linic printing. The writing is printed on the back to improve durability.

コンクリートづくりの電話ボックス。ポスターの掲示もできるようになっている。（チューリッヒ）

A concrete phone booth. Posters may be displayed, as well. (Zurich)

樹脂の特徴を生かした，内照式のサイン。

An inner lighting system sign taking advantage of the characteristic of resin.

コンクリートで個性的な空間を演出した例。（撮影：定村俊満）

An example showing how concrete can create a unique space. (Photographer: Toshimitsu Sadamura)

布も見逃せないサインの材料である。伝統的な表現方法で魅力的な例が多い。

Cloth is material that should not be overlooked, often used for signs.

ガラス張りの停留所。まちの景観がよく見えるように工夫されている。

A bus stop with glass walls. It is designed so that the town's scenery may be observed easily.

フイルム・シートは簡便でカラフルな素材として普及した。高輝度反射シートは自動車のヘッドライトの光に反射するので，道路標識としてもよく使われている。

Film sheets became popular because they are convenient and colorful. Reflective sheets reflect a car's headlights, and are often used for traffic signs.

手づくりの味を生かした陶板。フルカラー着色ができるのが魅力となっている。

A porcelain plate stressing handmade characteristics. Full-color printing is possible.

## 代表的な構造と特徴

### 1）壁面

　地面から垂直な壁のように立つサインで，立ったままの眼の高さとほぼ同じ高さの表示面を見る。表示面の大きさや文字の大きさによって多数の人が同時に見ることができる。このため利用者が集中する施設やイベントなどで使われることが多い。石やコンクリートを使ったものは重厚さがあり，安定感があって高価な印象を与える。反面重苦しく開放感に欠ける点もある。二本脚にパネルを付けたり，地面から板のようにパネルが立っているものは，軽快で洗練された印象を与えるが，安易で画一的なイメージにもなるので使う場所をよく考える。二本脚型やパネル型の軽量なものは腐食しやすく，表示面も通常の印刷では劣化しやすくなる。一般に街路での使用は景観と調和し風格と耐久性のある重量型が望ましい。施設内や短期間のイベントなどでは軽量型でもよい。

**Typical Structures and Features**

1) Wall-Type Signs

They are signs standing vertically upright from the ground like walls. Viewers, while standing, look at them which are generally placed on the same level as their eyes. Depending on the sizes of signs and letters on them, they can be seen by many people at the same time. This kind of signs is used at facilities and in the place of events where many people gather together. Signs made of stone and concrete give viewers a sense of depth and stability. They also give them the impression that they are costly. On the other hand, they look oppressive, and lack a sense of openness. Panels supported by a pair of legs and panels standing on the ground as if they are boards give a light and refined impression. Even so, when they are used, sites where they are put up must be chosen carefully so as to avoid causing a cheap and monotonous impression. The light-weight signs of the two-leg and panel types tend to rust quickly, and the surface of signs will easily deteriotate if an ordinary printing method is used. Generally speaking, in case wall-type signs are used on the street, heavy-weight type with durability and harmoneous with the scenery on the street is desirable. The light-weight type is alright for use inside facilities and at the site of events which are held for a short time.

壁型は拠点を意識的に表現する場合効果的な形態である。

The wall type is an effective form when the base is deliberately expressed.

壁型。多くの人が利用する施設に適切である。

Wall type. This type is appropriate for facilities used by many people.

## ２）斜面型

　表示面を斜めにするもので，小さなスペースで大きな表示面を得ることができる。現地と照合しやすく，視線に素直に対応して見やすくなる。視野が妨げられず，開放感があり，環境になじみやすい。しかし，比較的小型のサインに限られ，一度に多数の利用者に対応する必要があるものには向かない。石やコンクリートやレンガブロックでつくった量感のあるものとパネルを曲げた軽量感のあるものとがある。

## ３）平面型

　地面と水平な平面で表示するもので，地面に直接埋めこまれる例が多い。視覚的な障害にならず，現地の方位と完全に一致する表現ができる。景観との協調性は高いが，遠くからサインを発見するのが困難で，動線との一致や形の工夫が必要になる。ベンチのように立体化することもでき親しみやすいが，汚れやすい欠点がある。

2) Sloping Plane Type

The plane of signs is put up diagonally. With this, wide plane is obtained while they occupy small space. When this style is used, they correspond to areas smoothly, and it becomes easy for viewers to look at them. There is no obstacle to the field of vision and the there is a sense of openness. This type smoothly harmonizes with the environment surrounding areas. However, a comparatively small size only is suitable for this type of signs. This type is not good when signs must be seen by many persons simultaneously. There is a weighty type of signs made of stone, concrete and bricks, and also a light-weight type made by folding a panel.

3) Horizontal Type

Signs are shown on the plane which is placed horizontally with the ground. In most cases, they are buried onto the surface of the ground. This type does not obstruct one's vision and it is possible to use expressions which go completely with the bearings of the sites where signs are put up. They harmonize with the scenery of the sites, but it is hard to find them from a distance. Conformity with the flow of lines and designing contrivance will be required. It is also possible to use cubic structures like a bench. A shortcoming of this type is that signs become dirty soon.

分岐点では，動線と対向して注意を引き付ける。

At a junction, draw attention by opposing the path of flow.

斜面型は視界を妨げず，目の前に展開する景観と照合するのに便利である。

The slope type does not obstruct the view, and is convenient in comparing the scene in front of the viewer.

平面型。ベンチのような形にすることができ，人やまちの景観にもマッチするが，汚れやすくなるので，設置場所とメンテナンスを考慮してデザインしたい。

Flat type. These can be made in the shape of a bench, matching the human and town scenery well. However, they become dirty easily, so their positioning and maintenance must be considered when designing them.

## 4）柱型

棒状に立つサインで，場所をとらず軽快であるが，安易に立てられ繁雑な印象を与えることもある。破損しやすく，素材も限られるため，無表情で画一的になりがちである。郊外の広い空間や，自動車用サインに適当であり，また設置空間に余裕がなく下部を開けたいときに適当である。表示面の高さは通常「道路標識設置基準」に準じ，歩道上で2.5m以上，車道で4.5m以上開ける。

## 5）壁突出型

壁から突き出したサインで，袖看板，軒下看板，室内のロビーや道路の誘導や記名サインなどがある。動線と直交し視認しやすい。ただし，数が増えると重なり合って見にくくなる。手が届かない程度の高さに統一するとすっきりする。

## 6）壁付型

壁面に直接表示または平行に取り付けるもの。記名，タイトル，解説などを表示するものに多い。道路や通路と平行になる場合は近づかないと見えないが，煩雑化を避けられる。妥当な大きさとしてはできるだけ壁面と一体化させる。安易なものは環境の印象を悪化させるおそれがある。

### 4) Pillar Type

Sings which are erected like poles do not occupy much space, and give viewers a light impression. However, these signs, which can be erected so simply, sometimes cause a rough and coarse impression. They are breakable, and materials to be used for this type of signs are limited. For this reason, their designs tend to become expressionless and uniform. This type is good when used in open space in the suburbs of cities and as signs for use by automobiles. Also this type is appropriate when the space where they are set up is limited and when the lower part must be kept open. The level of these signs must be 2.5 meters or more above the sidewalks and 4.5 meters or more above the driveways, according to the "standards for the establishment of guideposts."

### 5) Protrouding type

This type of signs sticks out from walls. They are sideway signboards, signbords under the eaves, guiding signs in lobbies and on highways, registered signs, These signs, which vertically join the line of flow, can be easily seen. However, when too many signs of this type are put up together, they will lie one upon another, overlapping each other, and they cannot be seen clearly at first sight. If they are placed on the level which is beyond easy reach, there will appear a unified look.

### 6) Type Fixed to Wall

This type of signs is shown directly on walls or installed in parallel with walls. This type is mainly used for the showing of registered names, titles, comments, etc. in cases they are put up in parrallel with highways and passage ways, one cannot see them, unless he comes closer to them. Instead, they can avoid causing a disorderly look. When signs are made to create a sense of one-ness with the wall space, that will be a proper size. It is feared that if signs are designed in an easygoing way, they will worsen the impression of the environment.

柱型。シンプルで軽快な感じを与える。

Pillar type. A simple and cheerful feeling is achieved.

壁突出型。交通施設に多く用いられており，動線を明確に示すことができる。

Protruding type. This type is often used in transportation facilities, and can clearly convey the path of flow.

JR秋葉原のサイン。改良を加え空間のイメージを向上させている。

Sign at the JR Akihabara station. Reforms are being made to improve the image.

柱の絵で空間の楽しさを演出した例。

An example in which gaiety is expressed through the pictures on the pillar.

柱型は狭い場所にも設置できる。

Pillar types may be placed in limited spaces.

壁突出型。一般的な看板の一つだが，工夫次第で独創的になる。

Protruding type. Although a common form of sign, it is possible to design unique signs by being creative.

建物と一体化させ，装飾性と広告性を兼ねたサインとなっている。

The sign is unified with the building, acting both as a decoration and advertisement.

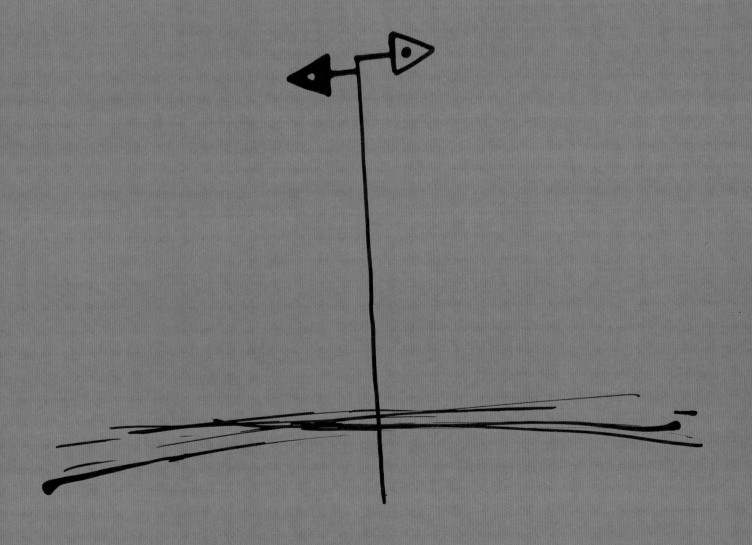

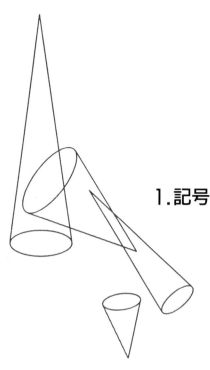

# 1.記号としてのストリート・ファニチュア

## Street Furniture as Symbols

石畳は独特の味わいがある。

This stone pavement has a unique atmosphere.

## 街路のイメージづくり

　人々は家の中だけでなく，屋外も生活空間の一部とし
て考えるようになった。屋外で快適に過ごすためには，
屋内と同じようにさまざまなファニチュアが必要になる。
ストリート・ファニチュアは，屋外空間を生活の場とし
て有効に活用していくための道具である。

　広い意味でサインもストリート・ファニチュアの一部
であり，またはストリート・ファニチュアもサイン的な
性格を持っていると考えられるが，ここではストリート・
ファニチュアをその目的と意味の側面からとらえ，まち
のイメージづくりのための一つの要素として考えてみた
い。

### Creation of Street Image

People have come to consider that not only
their homes but open space also is part of the space of
life. In order to enjoy outdoor life, various kinds of
street furniture are necessary, just as insider homes.
Street furniture is a tool needed for the effective use of
open space as the space of life.

Signs also are part of the street furniture in a
broad sense, while on the other hand, street furniture is
thought to have the nature which is something like
signs. In this Chapter, I want to think about street
furniture as one factor which creates a street image,
while giving light on its purpose and significance.

アーヘンの市庁舎前広場。ペーブメント・デザイン，
公衆電話，樹木，ベンチ，売店など広場に必要な設
備が配置されている。

Aachen city hall square. Facilities and objects
necessary for this kind of square, such as pavement designs, public telephones, trees, benches,
and shops, are located here.

石畳のパターンは，広い空間に変化を与える。

The patterns of stone pavement provide variety to large spaces.

空間は価値を生む。後ろ向きにコインを投げると幸運が訪れると信じられるようになった。(トレビの泉)

Space gives birth to value. It is believed that good luck will be obtained by throwing in a coin backwards. (Fontana di Trevi)

ペーブメントのパターンや起伏は，広場の重要なデザイン要素である。

The patterns and undulations of a pavement are important design elements of a square.

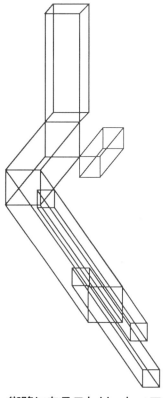

# 2. 人のための街路
**Street for People**

## 街路にあるストリート・ファニチュア

Street Furniture Seen on Streets

　道路のデザインの一部としてペーブメント・デザインがあるが，コストの関係で，手に入れやすい安価な素材が使われることが多かった。最近は，まちづくりはまず足元からという発想に支えられ，ペーブメント・デザインに力が入れられるようになったのは喜ばしい。天然石やレンガブロック，舗装タイルなど，多彩な素材が使われ，デザインもそのまちにふさわしいものが考えられつつある。しかし，滑りやすい，ハイヒールの踵がはさまって歩きにくいなどの苦情や問題提起もある。一方捨てられたチューインガムで汚され，処理しにくいという指摘もある。そのほとんどは利用者の道徳や公共のものを使うモラルの問題に帰する。すぐれたデザインでまちを美しく装うには，技術的な改善を行うほか，公共心を培う方法も考えていかなければならない。

　ペーブメントを構成する要素として，まちの個性を打ち出して行こうとする動きがあり，今まで気がつかなかったマンホールの蓋などにも目が向けられ，そのデザイン性が脚光を浴びている。

　下水道などはまちにとってなくてはならないものの一つであり，人とのかかわりが非常に深い。こうしたところにも目を向け，一般の人とのふれあいを大事にする意味も兼ね，デザインを一新している市町村が増えている。1986年，建設省と日本下水道協会が中心となって「下水道マンホール蓋デザイン20選」を選定し，下水道にも注目させる風潮が全国に広まっている。

**Street Furniture Seen on Streets**

　The design of pavements is part of the street designs. Low price materials easy to produce have been mainly used in order to reduce costs. It is welcomed that recently the designing of pavements is being made much of supported by the concept that city planning must start with pavements. Various kinds of materials are used, such as natural stone, brick blocs, tiles, etc. Pavements are designed so as to be harmonious with the feeling of towns. At the same time, however, problems are also arising, with pedestrians complaining that pavements are slippery, and that the heels of high-heeled shoes were caught in small holes in pavements. It is also pointed out that it is difficult to clean pavements which were soiled by chewing gums thrown away by pedestrians. Most of these problems concern pedestrians' morality and their way of using public facilities. Before beautifying towns with good designs, ways to foster a sense of public duty must also be studied, while carrying out technical improvement.

　There are moves to stress the characteristics of towns, as one factor which should be kept in mind while designing pavements. No one had so far paid attention to the design of manhole covers, but now they have started to show interest in them.

　Sewerage is indispensable for urban life. In view of its deep involvement in city life, many more cities, towns and villages are renewing the designs of manhole covers, taking an important view of connections with urban people in general. In 1986, the Construction Ministry and the Japan Sewerage Association selected 20 good designs for sewerage manhole covers in Japan. A trend for paying attention to the designing of sewerage is taking root nationwide.

ユニークなデザインで排水口とは思えない軽妙な味わいがある。

The unique design is witty, unlike typical overflows.

道路に面した擁壁の植栽は，無機的な面に潤いを与える。

The plantation of the protection wall facing the road provides charm to the otherwise in- organic surface.

スリップしないように工夫された坂道の石畳。

Stone pavement on a slope designed to prevent slipping.

木製のブロックの舗装は周囲の環境にやすらぎを与える効果がある。雨水で滑らぬよう木目を横方向に使うなど工夫すれば，すぐれた舗装材料になるだろう。(静岡県掛川市)

Wooden block pavements provide a sense of tranquility to the surrounding environment. By being creative, such as placing the grain of wood horizontally so that the blocks are not slippery when wet, this should become an excellent paving material. (Kakegawa City, Shizuoka Prefecture)

街角の芸術家が描いた街路の絵。道行く人を楽しませてくれる。

Street paintings by a street corner artist. They entertain people walking along the street.

## 道の管理とストリート・ファニチュア

　道路上には交通と都市の機能を円滑にする各種の管理にかかわる工作物が設置されているが，まちをすっきりと整理して景観をよくするため，電柱の埋設化が進められたり，路面にデザインを施したり，都市の環境を整備する事業が各地で行われている。

　そうした中で，信号機や電柱のカラー化が普及しつつある。そのすべてが好例とは言えないが，環境との調和を目指す有効な手段の一つとなっている。また，照明や案内標識の一体化が進み，次第にすっきりした町並みが形成されつつある。

　最近注目すべき二つの傾向がある。その一つは「人にやさしい街路」づくりを始めたことであり，もう一つは「公共空間の感覚」が育ってきたことである。車優先の発想から歩行者の快適性と歩行者優先の発想が出てきた。また，公共道路の照明器具やベンチなどから広告がなくなってきた。これは電柱広告や消火栓にも及びつつあり，都市の景観を整備して美しい町並みを目指す行政の積極的な施策として評価したい。

　環境への調和とまちのイメージづくりの一環として，工作物をイメージアップの小道具として採用する都市が増えている。その中に車止めがあるが，それも地域の環境，風物，産業，歴史などを表現するものをデザインの要素に採用しているところもある。こうしたところに心配りしたトータルなイメージづくりが，まちの景観を特徴あるもの，個性的なものにしていくのである。

### Control of Streets and Street Furniture

On Streets, various kinds of equipment are installed for the facilitation of control over traffic and city functions. In various cities, projects for arranging these installations neatly and improving the scenery of cities are being carried out. Now many telephone poles have been buried underground.

Most noted among these projects is the coloring of traffic signals and telephone poles. Some urbanites are not necessarily showing a favorable reaction to this, but his is one effective method of attaining harmony with the environment. Also the unification of the designs of lighting and guiding signs is progressing. Streets are gradually taking on a refined atmosphere.

Recently, two noteworthy trends are seen: One is the creation of "streets gentle for people" and the others is that "a sense about public open space" is growing up. The concept on giving precedence to pedestrians and protecting their comfort has started to take root, superseding the concept on giving precedence to automobiles. Also advertisements used to be seen on streets, such as on lighting apparatus and benches, are disappearing. This trend is also spreading as to advertisements on telephone poles and fire extinguishers for public use. We want to appreciate the government's positive policy for improving, by taking these measures, the scenery of streets.

An increasing number of towns are using public-use equipment as accessories for creating harmony with the environment and the image of a town. Public auto bumpers are one of the equipment used for that purpose. Some cities are using things, which represent the environment, scenery, industries, and history of their areas, as part of designs. This consideration, shown in creating an integrated image of towns, makes the scenery of their towns characteristic.

信号機の色彩も周囲に調和させるように工夫する傾向がある。

There is a tendency to design traffic signals so that the color blends in with the surrounding environment.

駅前のペーブメントの素材に合わせてデザインされた横断歩道は，周囲の景観ともマッチして美しい情景を作り出している。(静岡県掛川市)

The pedestrians' crossing, designed to match the material used for the pavement in front of the station, matches its surrounding, creating a beautiful scene. (Kakegawa City, Shizuoka Prefecture)

ガードレールは機能面だけでなくデザイン性も考えたい。

The design of guardrails should be considered, not only the functionality.

愛嬌がある消火栓。こうした楽しい消火栓を増やして行きたいものだ。

A charming and witty fire hydrant. We would like to see more fire hydrants with such fun designs.

京都市は電柱をカラー化してまちの景観と調和させている。

The city of Kyoto has assigned colors to the utility poles to harmonize with the city's scenery.

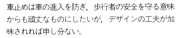

車止めは車の進入を防ぎ、歩行者の安全を守る意味からも頑丈なものにしたいが、デザインの工夫が加味されれば申し分ない。

Bumpers prohibit cars from entering, protecting pedestrians. For this reason, they should be sturdy, but it would be even better if designs were creative.

車の飛び込みを防ぐために設置された車止め。

A bumper preventing cars from rushing in.

# 道の照明

日本人は生活様式の中から，光に対して独特のセンスを磨いてきた。たとえば，障子に投影される光の微妙な趣や，行灯の明かりや欄間の光模様など，光に対して特別な感情を持っており，繊細な陰影を楽しんできた。ヨーロッパではステンドグラスのような彩りが愛されてきたが，文化の違いはあっても，古今東西，人はみな光に魅せられて生きてきたとも言える。

街路の照明はここ数年その進歩がめざましく照明器具の開発と，景観にマッチする照明の研究が進められ，光による景観の演出も行われるまで成長している。都市の照明は夜間の活動時間の延長に役立ち，防犯や治安の維持に欠かせない。また空間にシンボリックな意味を表現するライトアップをはじめ，照明は歴史やまちの個性を表現したり，都市にアクセントをつける役割を果たしている。

祭の光は，まちに潤いとエンターテインメントを与える要素の一つである。欧米ではクリスマスのシーズン，イルミネーションによってまちが彩られる。まちの明かりを考えるうえで，こうした祭の明かりのデザイン化は楽しい演出になるのではなかろうか。

灯籠，行灯，提灯，篝火，送り火，など長い歴史をもつ光が身近にある。日本人が昔から大切にしてきた繊細なあかりへの感覚を公共空間の中にも取り入れていきたいものである。

Japanese people have improved since old days a unique sense toward lighting used in their daily life. They have special fondness to delicate light reflected on shoji (sliding doors made of white paper), the shapes of light and shadows reflected on ranma (transoms) and the light of andon (portable paper-covered light stands). They have enjoyed delicate patterns haphazardly made by light and shadows. In Europe, people love stained glass. It can be said that even though there are differences in their culture, all people both in the East and the West have felt enchanted with light.

The lighting of streets has attained marked progress during the last several years. The development of lighting fixtures and study on lighting, which goes with the scenery on streets, have been carried out. So much so, even scenery is illuminated for the producing of stage effects. Lighting in towns helps prolong night-time activities, and is also essential for the prevention of crimes and protection of public security. Lighting gives a symbolic significance to open space, and also highlights the characteristics of towns and their history. It fulfills the role of giving an accent to towns.

Lighting at festivals is a factor which creates an emotion and the feeling of festivity in towns. In Western countries, towns are illuminated during the Christmas season. The designing of lighting used on these occasions will probably offer great enjoyment to people.

In Japan, there are many customs connected with light, such as toro (garden lanterns), andon, chochin (portable paper-covered light for outdoor use), kagaribi (bonfire), and okuribi (bonfire for escorting the spirit of the dead). We must preserve these traditions connected with light which Japanese people have valued for many years.

建物のイメージアップに役立ち，シンボルにもなっている照明。

Lights that improve the image of a building, acting as a symbol.

街路のデザインに調和した照明は，品のよさで町並みを引き立てる効果がある。

Refined lights that blend in with the street's design have the effect of enhancing the beauty of the city streets.

すぐれた装飾をした照明は雰囲気を高め，まちのアクセントにもなる。

Lights with superior decorations add atmosphere, acting as an accent of the city.

壁面に取り付けられた照明。建物の性格づくりに役
立っている。

Lighting fixtures on a wall. They have become
unique characteristics of the building.

伝統的な照明を使い親しみやすさと風格を演出して
いる。

By using traditional lights familiarity and character are expressed.

用賀プロムナードの照明。同じ素材を使い周囲の景
観に溶け込むよう工夫されている。(東京・世田谷区)

Lights at the Yoga promenade. They have been
designed using the same material so that they
blend in with their surroundings. (Setagaya
Ward, Tokyo)

ネオンサイン。賑わいのあるまちを感じさせるデザ
インになっている。(福岡市・中洲)

Neon signs. The design suggests the prosperity
of the town. (Nakasu, Fukuoka City)

## 道の演出

彫刻，噴水，遊具など道路に楽しさを演出するストリート・ファニチュアは数多く見られるようになった。

ヨーロッパでは町角に必ずと言ってもよいほど多様な彫刻が置かれている。日本にも昔は村や町のはずれにお地蔵さんや神社仏閣に彫刻があったが，街角にいわゆる彫刻が置かれるようになって日が浅い。芸術性が高く，人々を楽しませるウイットに富んだ彫刻となると，まだまだこれからの課題である。

ヨーロッパの町角ではどこに行っても噴水を見かける。水は人にとってオアシス的なやすらぎを引き出す。まちに潤いを持たせるためにも水の演出を大いに心掛けたいものである。

道路に置かれた遊具が，日本にはすくない。道路は遊び場ではないという感覚があり，これは都市の文化の問題であるかもしれないが，一考する余地がある。

遊具といってもブランコや滑り台を置くと言っているのではない。こどもたちは遊びの天才である。いろんなものを瞬く間に遊びの材料に変えてしまう。そういう遊びを触発するストリート・ファニチュアの出現を期待するのである。まちを散策するのが楽しくなるストリート・ファニチュアがあってもよい。最近都市の一角に昆虫が増えている。その昆虫を追って野鳥が訪れる例も増えている。日本全国ではいろいろ違いがあるかもしれないが，地域の特色や気候風土を考慮にいれれば，今まで気づかなかった鳥や小動物が棲息していることがわかるかもしれない。その他まちの歴史をたどったり，まちの産業や特徴を学んだりという，気軽な散策ができる空間づくりをしたいものである。こうしたところで，ちょっと一息いれられるストリート・ファニチュアの出現が待たれる。

Now we can see many street furniture, such as sculptures, fountains, sporting goods, etc., which bring forth an enjoyable atmosphere on streets.

In almost all street corners in Europe, various kinds of sculptures are displayed. In Japan in old times, stone images of Jizo were seen at the outskirts of towns and sculptures in shrines and temples. It is just recently in Japan that sculptures have been placed in the corners of streets. It will take some more time before Japan is able to put up witty sculptures which will be enjoyable to look at.

We can see fountains at street corners everywhere in Europe. Water gives people a sense of relief similar to that we feel when we seen an oasis. We must think about how to use water in order to create charming streets.

We can seldom see in Japan playthings placed on streets, because we have the concept that streets are not a playground. This may be a problem concerning urban culture, but the problem is worthy of study.

I am not insisting that swings and slides should be placed on streets. Children are genius as far as plays are concerned. They can instantly start playing with anything which they happen to find. I expect the appearance of street furniture which will stimulate the spirit to play. There should be street furniture which will make walking on streets more enjoyable. Recently, insects are returning to some cities, and accompanying their return, wild birds are also coming to cities. Situations in Japanese towns may not be the same. However, if we give thought to local characteristics and climates from another angle, we may realize that birds and small wild animals, whose presence we had not been aware of, have been living there. I want to create open space where one can take a walk light-heartedly, while examining the characteristics of a town and industries it has.

I am waiting for the appearance of street furniture which will let persons taking a walk on streets enjoy a brief rest.

ほのぼのとした彫刻。

Warm sculpture.

まちの彫刻には，芸術性と同時に人々に楽しさを与えるウィットに満ちたものであって欲しい。

It is necessary for sculptures in a city to be artistic and, at the same time, witty and entertaining.

篠栗88カ所の霊場を開いた一遍上人の像は，地域のシンボルとしても価値がある。

The statue of Ippen-Shonin, responsible for developing the 88 sacred places of Sasaguri, is valued as the district's symbol, as well.

橋げたから身を乗り出そうとしているカッパの姿はユーモラスであり，人々に歩く楽しさと話題を提供する。

The figure of the "kappa" (water imp) leaning over the bridge girder is humorous, providing pedestrians with entertainment and a topic of conversation.

イベントで設置された彫刻だが，都市空間に洒落た
彩りを添えている。

Although this is a sculpture placed here for a
special event, it has added a stylish air to this
urban space.

近くを通ると水が突然吹き出す彫刻。意外性があり
こどもたちや大人にも人気がある。こうした遊びが
都市の中にたくさん欲しい。

The sculpture suddenly spurts out water when
pedestrians walk by. Its unpredictability makes it
popular among children and adults alike.

地面から噴きでる小さな噴水と奥にある彫刻が，ま
わりの景観に品のよさを醸しだしている。

The small fountain and sculpture in the background create a refined scenery.

古い家の軒先を飾る彫刻は，人々の目を楽しませる。

The sculptures decorating the fronts of houses are entertaining.

路上で行われるチェス。そのアイデアが抜群である。

Chess being played on the street. The idea is excellent.

教会に飾られた怪物たちは，魔物を防いでいるように見える。

The monsters decorating the church appear to be protecting us against evil.

建物の壁についた噴水。小さいが観光客を楽しませる。

A fountain on a building's wall. Although small, it provides entertainment for tourists.

まちの中の彫刻

彫刻や噴水がまちのいたるところにあって，人々の
生活に潤いを与えている。観光客にとっても楽しい
演出となっており，まちを強く印象づけている。

Sculptures in the city.

Sculptures and fountains are found throughout
the city, adding charm to the lives of people there.
Tourists are entertained, as well, leaving a strong
impression of the city within them.

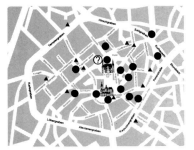

| | |
|---|---|
| ? インフォメーション | Information |
| ● 噴水・彫刻 | Fountain & Statue |
| ▲ 彫刻 | Statue |

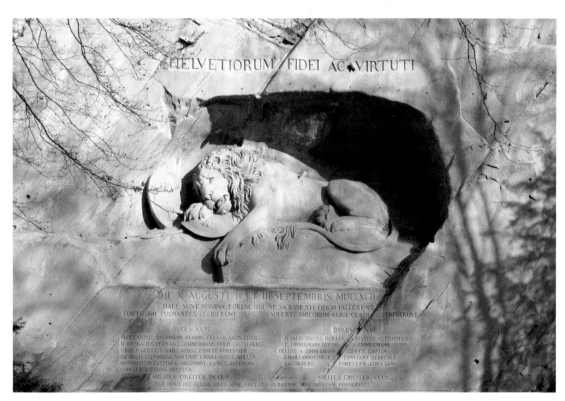

ルツェルンの「瀕死のライオン」は、スイス兵の勇敢さを讃えたものである。

The "Lion on the Verge of Death" in Luzern praises the bravery of the Swiss soldiers.

ライオンは眠らないという言い伝えがあり、不寝番の意味がある。今でも玄関のフェンスなどにその名残としてのデザインが見られる。

There is a legend that lions do not sleep, and are therefore associated with the meaning of a night watchman. We may still see the remains of this legend in the designs of lions on entrances and fences.

王のシンボルを使った王の聖堂。

The king's sanctuary using the king's symbol.

皇帝の象徴としての双頭の鷲はライオンと同じく権力の象徴であった。

The double-headed eagle symbolizes the emperor, and once had the same significance as the lion.

ライオンの噴水。ライオンは王家のシンボルであり、権威の象徴である。

A lion fountain. The lion symbolizes the royal family, and is symbol of power.

日本の神社にある狛犬（一対の獅子）は、「阿吽の呼吸」といって、気心が知れた関係を示し、「阿（あ）」は口を開いた形、「吽（うん）」は口を閉じた形になっている。

The lions seen in Japanese shrines represent the "a-un" (ahum: inspiration and expiration), symbolizing the understanding of each other. The "a" lion has the mouth open, and the "un" one closed.

天満宮でよく見かける牛は，知恵の神様や閻魔大王とのかかわりを示している。

Tho oows acon at the Tenmangu (shrine dedicated to Sugawara Michizane) express the relationship between figures such as the God of Wisdom and King of Hell.

渋谷パルコ前にある「NANAKO」は，日本で昔から親しまれてきた「招き猫」にユーモラスな表情をもたせた現代的な彫刻である。まちの新しい待ち合わせ場所となっている。

"Nanako" is located in front of the Shibuya Parco department store. It is a humorous and modern sculpture of the "Maneki-neko" (beckoning cat), which is traditionally a favorite among the Japanese people. It has become a new meeting place for the area.

ブレーメンの音楽隊にちなむ彫刻がブレーメン市庁舎の前にあり，まちの物語りを伝えている。

Sculptures representing Bremen's musical band is placed in front of the city hall, conveying the story of the city.

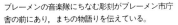

狼と赤ずきんの童話を扱った彫刻。

Sculpture portraying the story of Little Red Riding Hood.

食物がないため，自分の胸を突き，その血をこどもたちに飲ませる白鳥の姿。博愛のシンボルとなっている。

A figure of a mother swan stabbing her own breast to feed her starving children with her blood. This has become a symbol of philanthropy.

ライン選帝侯の中心都市として栄えたハイデルベルグのカール・テオドール橋の下にあった，証文と小さなネズミの像。日本でもネズミは富の象徴である。

The statuses of a deed and small mouse under the Karl-Theodor Bridge in Heidelberg a city which prospered as the center of the Rhein Kurfurst. Mice symbolize wealth in Japan, as well.

鹿の角は薬になったところから，今でも薬局のシンボルとして使われている。

Since deer horns have been historically used as medicine, they are still used as a symbol of drug stores.

鳩は自由と博愛の象徴であり，薬局のシンボルとしても使われている。

The pigeon is a symbol of philanthropy, and is used as a symbol of drug stores.

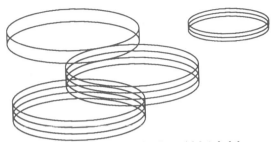

# 3.まちの快適性

**Adding Comforts to Town**

天然の石はベンチにもなる。

Natural rocks become benches, as well.

## ベンチ，ごみ箱

### Benches and Trash Cans

バス停，ポケットパークなどには待合や休憩のためのベンチが必要である。広場や街路にもベンチが欲しい。ベンチは耐久性があって，その場に似合い，使いやすい形状であるのがデザインの条件である。歩道が狭くてベンチを置くスペースが確保しにくい場合は，軽く寄りかかれる程度のベンチでもいい。ポケットパークや待合場所などでは，落ち着いて腰を降ろせる低いタイプのものが望ましい。素材は，いつでも安心して使える耐久性があるものがよく，汚れを落としやすく清潔で，座って心地よい感じがするものならなおよいと思う。

ベンチに近接して設置されるものにごみ箱がある。屋外で出すごみは各人が持ち帰るのが原則であり，安易にごみ箱を設置するのはあまり賛成できないが，交通の拠点や大型の施設や自動販売機の周辺には必要だろう。ごみ箱のデザインはその場所を考えた末のデザインとして，一工夫してもらいたい。使い勝手がよいのは，耐久性があり，回収しやすい，投入口が小さい（15cmぐらい），肩が丸い形，ごみ箱の底を浮かせて設置してあるものなどである。

吸い殻入れは，待合場所や休憩する空間など人が滞留する場所に設置する。ごみ箱と一体化したものがあるが，その区別があいまいで，感心できない。ベンチと一体化したものも周囲に不潔感を与えるので好ましくない。

It is necessary to place benches at bus stops and in small parks for use by people who want to sit down while waiting for buses or while resting. It will be desirable if there are benches at plazas and on the streets. Durable materials should be used for public-use benches, and they must be made easy to handle. They also must match with the places where they are placed. These are conditions required when benches are designed. If space on the street is limited for placing benches, small benches, which just permit persons to lean against them lightly, will be good enough. In small parks and waiting places, low benches where people can sit down and relax are desired. It will be much better if benches are made of materials which are durable, easy to remove dirt, and comfortable to sit down.

Trash cans are usually placed close to benches. In principle, people are requested to take trash home when they go out. For this reason, it is not advisable to place trash cans casually in public places. However, it is probably necessary to provided them at traffic key points, large-scale facilities, and areas where vending machines are installed. Trash cans should be designed, while taking into account what types of cans will be suitable for areas where they will be placed. When durable materials are used for trash cans, and when they have small openings (about 15 cm) and round shoulders, it will be easy to collect trash inside cans. Also, there should be some space between the bottom of cans and the ground.

Ash trays should be set up in waiting rooms and others places where many people gather. Some ash trays are combined with trash cans, and the two functions are not clearly separated. This type is not recommended.

木の切株は自然がくれたベンチでもある。

Tree stupms are benches from nature.

人が集まるところに設置されたベンチであるが、外向きになっており、お互いを干渉しない、ほどよい距離が保たれている。

These benches were placed where many people gather, but since they face outward, enough distance is maintained for privacy.

ベンチの基本的な条件を満たしている。つやと光りて管理が行き届いていることがわかる。

The basic conditions for a bench have been met. The luster proves that they have been maintained well.

見どころに置くベンチは設置場所を十分検討した上で設置する。これに付随するゴミ箱の位置と形も工夫したい。

The location of benches that are placed in prominent spots must be considered carefully. The design and location of the accompany trash cans must also be planned with care.

遊具としても使えるベンチ。（撮影：定村俊満）

Benches that children can play on, as well. (Photographer: Toshimitsu Sadamura)

用賀のベンチ。周囲の景観も重視している。

Benches in Yoga, Tokyo. Attention has been paid to the surrounding scenery, as well.

寄り掛かれるベンチ。都会の街路では腰をおろせる
ベンチよりも，ちょっと寄り掛かれるベンチの方が
機能的でもあり，清潔でもある。

Benches to lean on. On city streets it is often
more functional and sanitary to have benches
that may be leaned on, rather than sat on.

建物につけられたベンチ。視覚的なアクセントとな
っており，道行く人にも親切な配慮が感じられる。

Benches attached to a building. They are a visual
accent. Consideration is shown to pedestrians, as
well.

広場の彫刻。ベンチとしても使われ親しまれている。
（朝倉響子作）

Popular sculptures in a square that may be used
as benches, as well. (Artist: Kyoko Asakura)

高級感があるゴミ箱の一つだが，ゴミが見えないよ
うにし，ゴミを入れやすいように工夫すべきだろう。

Although it is a high class trash can, it would be
better to design it so that the contents are not
visible, and so that it is easier to throw away the
trash.

回収しやすさを考えたゴミ箱。汚れにくいがビニー
ル袋が露出しないよう工夫したい。

Collection is made simple with this trash can.
Although it keeps it clean, it would be better to
design the can so that the plastic bag does ot
show.

東京でよく見かけるステンレスのゴミ箱とたばこの吸い殻入れは、スリムでゴミがみえにくく、清潔感があるデザインである。

The stainless steel trash cans and ashtrays that can often be found in Tokyo are slim, clean, and sufficiently hide the contents.

大きなゴミ箱も入れ口が小さく、肩が丸く下が絞られており、軽快な感じがする。蓋の色も清潔な感じとなるよう工夫されている。

The openings are small even on large trash cans, the upper corners are rounded, and the body narrows down at the towards the bottom, resulting in a light, fun design. The color of the lid makes it look sanitary.

入れ口が小さく、肩が丸くなっており、照明器具やフェンスなどにも取り付けられている。ゴミが見えないいないように工夫され、下から回収できる構造である。ヨーロッパの街角ではこうしたタイプがよく使われている。

The opening is small, and the corners rounded. They may be attached to lighting fixtures and fences. The trash cannot be seen, and can be collected from the bottom. This type is often used in European cities.

必要な場所に、利用しやすい形で配置するよう心掛けたい。

It is important to place them in needed locations, in shapes that are easy to use.

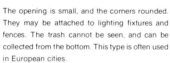

街路の水飲みは少ない。清潔に保ちメンテナンスを考えて設置する必要がある。

There are few drinking fountains on city streets. It is necessary to consider sanitation and maintenance when placing them.

日本でも伝統的な水飲みや噴水がある。すぐれたデザインのものが多い。

There are many traditional drinking fountains and water fountains in Japan. Many are of excellent design.

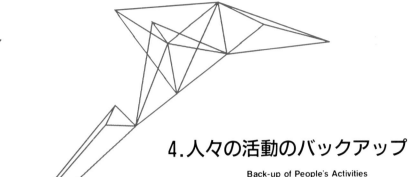

# 4.人々の活動のバックアップ

**Back-up of People's Activities**

## トイレ

Toilets

　ストリートファニチュアとして比較的大きなものに，トイレ，電話ボックス，交番などがある。臭い，汚い，こわいの3Kと言われていた公共のトイレも最近はきれいで清潔になってきた。フランスにおけるカプセル型のトイレが開発されたのを契機に，この数年の間に機能も改善され，デザインも工夫された美しいトイレが見られるようになった。トイレの内外ともに品質も高くなり，清潔である。今後も公共のトイレについては，機能とデザインに対する研究を行い，全国いたるところにすぐれたトイレが設置されるように努力していただきたい。

　　　Public toilets, telephone booths, and police boxes are comparatively large-size street furniture. Public toilets, which had been notorious for their bad smelling, filthiness, and fearfulness, are becoming clean. With the development of capsul-type public toilets in France as a turning point, the functions of toilets have been improved. Clean public toilets with good designs are now appearing in many places, and high quality materials are also being used for their interior and exterior. Study must be conducted on the functions and design of public toilets henceforth, aiming to build good toilets all over Japan.

最近トイレは，臭い，汚い，暗い，危険の4Kといわれたイメージを一新しつつある。

Restrooms are becoming cleaner, safer, and brighter.

パリのカプセル型のトイレ。まちの中に設置されトイレの概念を変えたが，景観との調和を考えれば建築物の中に設置して通りからも自由に入れるようにしたいものである。

A capsule-shaped toilet in Paris. Although this is a change in the concept of restrooms in the city, if considering the harmony with the surrounding environment, it would have been best to place the restrooms in a building, allowing access from the street.

明るい色で形を工夫したトイレ。床面の素材を変えれば清潔感が増すだろう。

A bright restroom in a creative shape. It would appear more sanitary by using a different material for the floor.

# 電話ボックス

地域の特徴を生かした個性的な電話ボックスが設置されている。NTT の量産タイプのものから，周辺の景観にマッチするオリジナル・デザインのものまで，かなりバラエティがある。世界的な規模で眺めると，各国ともそれぞれ個性がある。これからの国際化社会を考慮した，文化的にもすぐれた電話ボックスの出現を期待している。

## Telephone Booths

Telephone booths designed to symbolize the characteristics of areas, have been installed in many places. There are a variety of designs for public telephones, starting with mass-produced NTT telephones to telephones which are original in design and harmonize with the scenery of the areas where they are set up. The designs of public telephones in foreign countries are unique. I hope that telephones with high cultural levels will be designed to meet internatinalization of society.

ドイツの頑丈な電話ボックス。

A sturdy German telephone booth.

粋な形をしたローマの電話。

A chic telephone in Rome.

ホテル・ニューオオタニに設置されている電話ボックス。日本的なイメージが周囲の景観にも調和している。

Telephone booth found in the Hotel New Otani. The Japanese image matches the surrounding scenery.

ロンドンの電話ボックス。

Telephone booth in London.

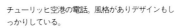

チューリッヒ空港の電話。風格がありデザインもしっかりしている。

Telephone in the Zurich Airport. There is character, and the design is impressive.

パリの電話ボックス。大胆なガラス張りになっている。

Telephone booth in Paris. The design is bold, with glass walls.

どっしりと落ち着いた感じのある電話。

A telephone with a dignified presence.

ミラノ空港内の電話。右下に吸い殻入れがついており，イメージ・カラーの黄色が印象的である。

Telephone in the Milano Airport. An ashtray is attached to the lower righthand corner, and the image color of yellow is impressive.

存在感があるどっしりした形。（イギリス）

The shape has a dignified presence. (England)

機能的なポスト。（ドイツ）

A functional mailbox. (Germany)

建物と一体化したポスト。（スイス）

A mailbox unified with the building. (Switzerland)

民家で使われていたポスト。階段にも住む人のこだわりが感じられる。

A mailbox used in a private home. The stairs convey the inhabitants' philosophy.

## 交番

　治安と防犯，地理案内など，まちと警察との接点になる交番が，個性化しつつある。まちにとって重要な役割を果たす施設であり，外国にはない警察のシステムとして，海外からも注目されている。サイン的にみると「さくら」のマークは外人には理解しがたいようである。交番としてすぐわかるマークやサインに改めたいものである。

### Police Boxes

Police boxes are a meeting point between the police and town people. They are the key point which maintains the public security of towns, prevents crimes, and supplies information on locations. The design of police boxes is becoming more original. They fulfill an important role for town dwellers. Feign countries, which have no police box system, are watching Japan's police boxes with interest. However, foreigners are puzzled by the cherry blossom mark, the symbol of police boxes, and wonder what it signifies. A mark or sign which can be understood by any person at first sight ought to be adopted.

交番。美しく，親しみがもてるデザインになっている。桜のマークは外国から来た人に理解されにくいので，遠くからもよく見えるマークにしたい。

A police box. The design is beautiful and warm. It is difficult for foreigners to recognize and comprehend the cherry blossom logo, so it should be something that can easily be seen from a distance.

赤坂に設置されたインフォメーション・センターは，新しい検索システムを備えており，今後の展開が楽しみである。

The information center located in Akasaka is equipped with a new reference system.

世界の海の玄関といわれるロンドン橋。

The London Bridge is said to be the entrance to the world's seas.

昔からある橋は堂々としており，まちの風格を高めている。（ベルン）

The old bridge has presence, adding to the character of the city. (Bern)

掛川駅の地下通路は明るく爽やかである。白っぽい色彩で光の反射を利用し，壁面もさりげなく装飾されている。

The underground passage at Kakegawa Station is bright and pleasant. Near-white colors have been used to reflect the light, and the wall decorations have been kept simple.

個性的な橋は人々の心の中に生きつづける。（小田原市・学橋）

The unique bridge has left a lasting impression in people's minds. (Manabu Bridge, Odawara City)

現代の橋。横断歩道橋は交通安全の上からは必要かもしれないが，機能だけでなく美的感覚も充足する方向で考えるべきである。

A modern bridge. Although pedestrian bridges are necessary from a safety standpoint. They should be designed to be attractive as well as functional.

歩行者専用の橋。周囲の景色をのんびり楽しめる雰囲気を備えている。これからの橋をデザインする上での一つの方向として検討する余地がある。

A bridge for pedestrians. It has an atmosphere encouraging people to enjoy the surrounding scenery. It should be studied as an example of a future direction of bridge designs.

# 時計

時計は古くから建物や空間のなかに設置され，まちの象徴として親しまれてきた。ヨーロッパでは中世の街角に置かれた日時計や駅の大時計などがあり，時を告げるという本来の目的よりも，まちを彩るイメージアップや演出効果の役割が注目されている。

## Clocks

Since old times, people have had a friendly feeling to clocks set in the front of buildings and clock towers which are something like the symbol of towns. In Europe, in the corner of streets, there are sundials set up in the medieval age and big clocks at stations. Their role of creating stage effect and improving the image of towns is regarded more important than their function as the machine to tell time.

海上施設にふさわしい遊び心豊かな時計。モダンな施設と調和している。（福岡市）

A fun and witty clock suitable for this marine facility. It is harmonized with the modern facility. (Fukuoka City)

街角に時計が多く，お国柄を表している。

The many clocks found in the city convey the characteristics of the country.

石組も美しい風格のある文字板。

Refined sign board with beautiful stonework.

悠久の時の流れを感じさせる日時計。

A sundial giving the impression of the passing of time.

美しい文字板。

Beautiful sign board.

観光の名所メーアスブルクの門につけられた時計。植物も美しくまちを彩っている。（ドイツ）

A clock on the famous Meersburg gate. The plants add to the beauty of the town. (Germany)

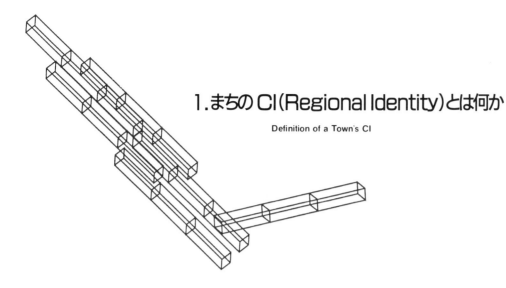

# 1.まちのCI(Regional Identity)とは何か

## Definition of a Town's CI

## CIの意味

CIとは「コーポレート・アイデンティティ」を略したことばで、企業活動のビジョンを明確にし企業内外に向けて的確なイメージをつくり、社会的な存在価値を高めていくための体系的なコミュニケーション計画のことである。

まちのCIはコーポレート・アイデンティティの概念を取り入れたもので、「コミュニティ・アイデンティティ」や「シティ・アイデンティティ」の略であるとされている。企業が行っているのと同じように、まちの一体的かつ計画的なイメージづくりをしようというものである。本来これは「RI＝リージョナル・アイデンティティ」と呼ばれるべきで、著述や講演においてRIと語ってきたが、最近では一般にCIと言う方が意味が通じやすくなった。ただし、外国人にはまちのCIと言っても通用しない。リージョナル・アイデンティティと言う方が適切である。

まちのCIは、共同体としてのイメージアップを図る上で、またまちのシンボル・マークやロゴタイプを刷新したりする表現上、企業のCIと似ているが、人が住む快適な環境や、生涯にわたって生活する視点で考えた場合、大きな違いがある。

CIは基本的には住民対策、観光対策、地域産業対策などの各種事業を体系化し発展させるものである。CIによって事業の効率化や個性化を図るとともに、住民一人ひとりのまちに対する愛着や誇りを育て、このまちに住んでよかったと実感させることにもつながる。また、対外的にはまちの豊かなイメージをアピールし、歴史的、文化的にすぐれたまちであることを強調する目的もある。

## CIの必要性

まちのCIは、マークを制定したりサインを設置したり、便箋や封筒のデザインを統一したり、まちで使っている車両のデザインを変えるといった視覚的なCIを行なうという認識だけでは不十分である。

その基本としてまちづくりの理念と総合的なビジョンを据え、広範囲なデザイン計画とイメージづくりに沿った具体的な方策を体系的に整理すべきである。マークやデザインはその結果であって、目的ではない。このようにまちのCIと取り組む姿勢を明確にしておくべきであろう。

したがってまちのCIは、デザインやイベントや産業振興やまちのインフラストラクチャーまでの一貫した理念の追及の結果が総合的にまとめられていくと理解すべきである。

まちでCIに取り組む効用は、セクショナリズムに陥りがちな縦割りの行政事務機構を超え、横断的な関係と有機的な結束が図られる点である。現実にまちのCIを計画し完成させたまちの多くが、行政マンの意識の改革に役立ち、制度や行政機構の改革に役立っている例が多い。

こうした効用を考えれば、単にCIを計画通りにつくるというだけではなく、幅広い分野から横断的に人材を選び、お互いの立場や役割を理解し合い、共通の理念やコンセプトに練り上げて行くプロセスが非常に重要である。そうした意味でCI計画委員会を位置付けていただきたい。

それを敷衍して言えば、まちのCIは他の市町村のすぐれた事例を形通りに移し、画一的に無難な線で短期間にまとめるのではなく、そのまちのアイデンティティとは何かを考えた、他の市町村とは一味も二味も違う個性的なCIへと練り上げていかねばならない。

## CI計画の作業

作業に当たって、まず最初に理念やコンセプトを練り上げるべきだと書いたが、それを実現する具体的な組織は「CI委員会」「サイン策定委員会」などのような、実務責任者レベルの委員会をつくるのも一案である。まちのCIの基礎となる実情を徹底的に調べ、箇条書きにまとめてみる。まちにはいたるところにその材料が転がっている筈である。材料のすべてを出し尽くしたところで、CIにとって不要なものを消去していけば、最終的に残ったものがエッセンスになる。そのエッセンスを具体的な形としてどのようにデザインするかを次の段階で追及していくとよい。

最初から業者まかせにするのではなく、専門的な立場でのアドバイスを受けながらも、そのまちにふさわしいCIとはいったい何かを絶えず追及する態度を持ちつづければ、必ずやまちのCIは個性豊かなものとして完成していくに違いない。そこには副次効果としての思いがけない発見もある。

筆者もいくつかの事例にアドバイザーとして参加したが、成功例に共通するのは、自分たちのまちのCIは自分たちの手づくりに近い形でまとめるのだという結束であった。専門家は専門的な立場からのヒントを与えたり、その方向を間違えないように支えることだと痛感した。

## CIの事例と成果

福岡県立花町はとりたてて知られたものは何もない、ありふれたまちだった。ここではCI計画とサイン計画を平行して実施したが、まちの理念やコンセプトが明確になったため、具体的なまちづくりがスムーズに進行している。それによってまち全体が明るくなり、イメージアップにつながっている。これが先進的な事例の一つとして評価されており、視察に訪れる他の市町村が増え知名度も上がり、まちの人たちが愛着と誇りを持つまでになっている。イメージ・チェンジとしても成功した例である。

青森県下田町は基地の町三沢に近い小さな町であるが、CI委員会によって「しーもくん」がかわいいマスコット・キャラクターとして制定され、みごとにまちの外交官として活躍している。

こうした成功事例は枚挙の暇もないくらいであるが、思いつくままに北から順に上げてみると、小樽のまちの運河を中心とする町並み整備、盛岡市の城址公園から見える景観の保全、仙台市の「杜の都」づくりへの市民のコンセンサス、横浜市の馬車道通りの先進的な地域づくり、掛川市における地元の産物を個性化した「これっしか処」、神戸市の外国人がひとり歩きできる街づくり、福岡市のアジアの拠点都市としてのまちづくり活動など、テーマも展開方法も多彩である。

大分県の一村一品運動は、県知事の哲学が地域の産業起こしにつながった著名な例である。これらはCIとは呼べないかもしれないが、日本の社会に大きな影響を及ぼしたという意味で、形を変えたCI的な事例である。

要するにまちづくりとイメージ計画は、そのまちにあるあらゆる資源を見直し、まちをあげて一致協力していけば、成し遂げられる事業なのである。各種の事業を散発的に行うのではなく、事業を統括する明確なコンセプトがあって、それを具体化していく知恵が生まれれば、個性的なまちづくりができるのである。

## Definition of CI

CI stands for "corporate identity." This is a systematic communications plan with the aim of drawing up enterprises' clear image on behalf of persons outside and inside enterprises, by showing their activities clearly, and thus increasing the significance of their social existence.

A town's CI has adopted the concept of corporate identity. It is said that a town's CI is the abbreviation of "community identity" or "city identity." Its purpose is to formulate a unified and systematic image of a town just as enterprises are doing. This idea should essentially be called "RI," or regional identity. I have been referring to it as "RI" in my books and speeches. Recently people have come to understand CI more easily than RI. However, foreigners will not understand a town's CI. It is appropriate to refer to it as regional identity.

The purpose of a town's CI is to improve the image of a community and to reform a town's symbol marks and logotype. In this sense, it is similar to enterprises' CI. However, there are big differences between them, if a town's CI is viewed from the standpoint of creating a comfortable environment where people want to live for life.

The basic purpose of a town's CI is to develop systematically a town's various projects, such as measures related to town people, tourism, local industries, etc. CI will help towns carry out town projects effectively and give them originality. At the same time it will foster town people's love and pride toward their towns. This will eventually have them realize the benefit of living in their towns. Another purpose of CI is to appeal to people living outside the town on the good image the town has, and to stress to them its cultural and historical prominence.

## Formulation of CI Plan

I stressed that before drawing up a CI plan, it is necessary to polish up first an idea and concept. It is advisable to establish a committee of administrative officials responsible, such as a "CI committee," of a "sign designing committee." Thorough surveys should be carried out on actual situations of a town, which will become the basis of CI, and the outcome of such surveys should be itemized. Town must be full of materials which should be taken up in CI. When all possible materials are collected, they should be eliminated from what is less important, and the materials which are left uneliminated to the last will become the essence. At the next stage, study should be conducted on how to design this essence concretely.

The drafting of a town's CI should not be left to enterprises from the beginning. If a town upholds the attitude of persistently pursuing the problem of what is a best CI for the town, while seeking advice from experts, it will certainly be able to accomplish its CI as a project which is full of originality. In that process, there will be unexpected by-effect discoveries.

I have participated in several town's CI projects in the capacity of an advisor. All towns which carried out the projects successfully were united by the idea that they will draw up their CI with their own hands. I realized from this that experts' task is to give suggestions from their position as experts and to support towns, so as to prevent them from heading for a wrong direction.

まちの境界や施設などの境界は，来訪者の印象を左右する重要なデザイン要素である。

The city boundaries and facility boundaries are important design elements affecting the impression of visitors.

## Need of CI

If one is to understand that CI's task is to decide marks, set up signs, unify the designs of letter paper and envelops used by a town, change the designs of cars a town is using, in other words, if he is to grasp that CI's tasks concern a visual field only, that will not be enough.

On the basis of a town-building concept and a comprehensive vision, concrete measures should systematically be arranged, in line with a wide-range design plan and an image creation. Marks and designs come after that; they are not the purpose. An attitude toward CI should be made clear first of all.

Accordingly, we should understand a town's CI as the process of comprehensively unifying the result of the integrated pursuit of concepts concerning designs, events, the promotion of a town's industries and infrastructure.

In the course of drawing CI, a town will be able to overcome administrative sectionalism, and establish overall and organic unity. Many towns, which planned and completed CI successfully, have been able to reform administrative official's awareness and the town's administrative system and structure.

If these effects are considered, it is more important to go through the process of selecting able personnel from extensive fields, of understanding each official's position and duties, and of polishing up CI as a concept to be shared by them in common, rather than to merely draft CI just as planned. I hope that the CI planning committee's position will be understood, in this respect.

If I can say further, a town's CI should not be drawn up from a uniform, conservative, and short-range viewpoint, by merely following suit after other town's successful examples. Efforts should be made to formulate a town's CI which will be unique and quite different from other towns.

## Examples of CI and Results

Tachibana Town in Fukuoka Prefecture is just an ordinary commonplace town which has no characteristic especially. But the town carried out its CI and design plans at the same time. After it set forth the clear idea and concept about how the town should be,

the building of the town is making headway smoothly and concretely. With this, the whole town has become animated, and its image has also improved. Many towns and villages are inspecting Tachibana Town, appreciating the results attained by this pioneer town. Inhabitants of Tachibana Town are coming to love the town and take pride in it. This is one example which shows how a town succeeded in changing its image.

Shimoda Town in Aomori Prefecture is a small town located close to Misawa, a US military base in Japan. The CI Committee of the town invented "Shiimo-kun," the mascot of the town. It has become very popular even outside the town. The mascot has become a diplomat of the town.

There are a countless number of successful cases throughout Japan. If I casually cite whatever cases coming into my mind, and if I start from the northern part of Japan, there is the case of Otaru which remodeled streets along a canal; Morioka City which has preserved the scenery viewed from the park built in the site where there was an ancient castle; Sendai City which obtained city people's consensus for the creation of the "forest city;" Yokohama City which tackled the establishment of an avant-garde area on the Bashamichi Street; City of Kakegawa which placed on the market "Koresshika-dokoro," by giving originality to one of its local products; Kobe City which changed part of its streets so that foreigners can visit there by themselves, not accompanied by Japanese speaking people; and Fukuoka City which established itself as Japan's key city toward Asia. Their themes and ways of developing their ideas are diversified.

Oita Prefecture's one-local-product-for-one-village movement is noted as an example whereby the governor's philosophy resurrected the prefecture's industries. These cases may not come under CI, but they are similar to it, in that they brought about big influence on Japanese society.

Town building and image projects will be carried out successfully, if towns examine once again the resources they have and if towns as a whole cooperate for the utilization of their resources. If they have a unified clear-cut concept and wisdom to unify various kinds of projects for building towns and carry them out organically, they will be able to create towns which will be full of originality.

広場。フレシキブルで快適な空間とするには，スト
リート・ファニチュアなどにも力を入れて整備する。

Square. In order the create a flexible and pleasant
space, it is important to place emphasis on equipment such as street furniture.

まちの中心的な部分を重点的に整備し印象づけると
ともに，情報が集中するように工夫する。

The design concentrates on equipping the center
of town, giving it a strong impression, making
sure that information gathers there.

道路。今まで機能が重視されていたが，最近では景
観上の配慮が加えられるようになり，美しい町並み
が演出されている。

Road. Although function was emphasized until
now, we have recently been seeing more consideration towards the scenery, creating beautiful
towns.

公園。人々が心身ともにリフレッシュできる空間に
するには，身近なところで活用できる親しみやすい
個性的な場所でありたい。

Park. In order to create a space allowing people to
refresh their body and soul, it is important to make
a unique and warm area, close enough to easily
utilize.

装飾。建物や広告などにも、地域全体の魅力を高めるようなコンセンサスが得られるように、行政としても働きかけることが重要である。

Decorations. It is important for the administration to take part in reaching a consensus to increase the charm of the entire district through buildings and advertisement.

構造物の材質。地域の風土や文化を生かす素材は環境とも調和する。

Materials of structures. Materials taking advantage of the district's climate and culture harmonize with the environment.

水はまちの景観になくてはならぬデザイン要素である。朝倉町の3連水車は約200年前から14ヘクタールの田圃を潅漑しつづけている。今ではまちの主要な観光のポイントになっている。

Water is a design element essential to the town's scenery. The three-row water mill of Asakura has continued to irrigate the 14-hectare rice fields for the past 200 years. It has now become an important tourist attraction.

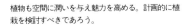

植物も空間に潤いを与え魅力を高める。計画的に植栽を検討すべきであろう。

Plants add charm to a space. Plants should be planned and evaluated.

サインの基本的な役割は，自分のアイデンティティ
を示すことである。あらゆる要素がその人の特徴に
なる。

The basic role of a sign is to convey one's own
identity. A variety of elements becomes that person's characteristics.

歴史と文化。まちの景観は長い歴史や人々の文化と
の関係で形成されている。アーヘン工科大学マンフ
レッド・シュパイデル教授の日乾煉瓦による建築実
習。

History and culture. A town's scenery is formed
by the relationship between long histories and
culture. This is a sun-baked brick architectural
training course conducted by TH. Aachen Pros.
Manfred SPeidel.

自然の景観。アウトバーンの休憩所からの眺めは，
ありふれた中にも自然の魅力を感じさせる。

Natural scene. The view from the Autobahn's rest
area is common, but we are able to appreciate the
beauty of nature.

ストリート・ファニチュア。椅子や舞台や布や彫刻
がシンプルな空間の魅力を高めている。

Street furniture. Items such as chairs, stages,
cloth, and scupltures increase the charm of a simple space.

京都の建物。地域の素材，風土，歴史文化などの密
接な関係がわかる。

A buildig in Kyoto. We are able to understand the
close relationship between the district's materials,
climate, history, and culture.

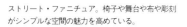

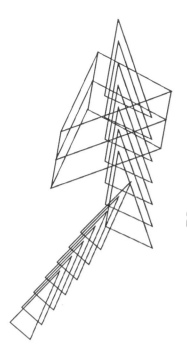

タイトルサイン　Title sign

# 2. CI 計画の基本

Basics of a CI Plan

## スローガン

「梅栗つくってハワイに行こう」とは大分県大山町が掲げたスローガンである。「学問の太宰府」もなかなか強烈なイメージ戦略であった。このようにスローガンは，簡潔で覚えやすく，地域の特色を一言で表現できるものがよい。スローガンは，さまざまな計画の基本理念としてまちの目標を示し，方針を統一させることができる。

## グラフィックシンボル

まちのグラフィックシンボルには，町章，シンボルマーク，キャラクターマーク，ピクトグラムなどがある。町章とシンボルマークは本来同一のものであるが，古い町章を今まで通りに残しながら，現代的で一般にアピールしやすいシンボルマークを制定する市町村が増えている。

## 色彩

イメージ色を明確に制定するまちもある。青森県下田町の「にんじんの赤」，「田園の緑」，「空の青」は，まちの産物や緑深い情景，高く澄み渡った大空などが連想される，説得力のある色の制定である。

## ネーミング

スローガンと同様，ネーミングは非常に重要なファクターである。京都の「哲学の道」，福岡の予備校に通じる道や，川崎市の競輪場に通ずる道が「親不孝通り」などと一般に呼ばれているのは，秀逸な例である。最近では東京・原宿の「ブラームスの小径」が話題になった。新しくネーミングするときは公募する例が多いが，幅広く調査し，専門家の意見を加えることも必要である。ネーミングの対象としては道路，公園，施設，物産などがある。

## ロゴタイプ

ロゴタイプは町名などの専用文字として使われ，町の個性を表現する。タイプフェイスは文書などの標準書体として一貫して使用する。これらを統一的に使えば，美しい表現となり，まちのイメージをアピールできる。

Slogan

"Let's grow apricots and chestnuts, and then let's go to Hawaii!" This is a slogan put up by Oyama Town, Oita Prefecture. "Dazaifu of learning" — this is also a forceful image strategy. These slogans are simple and easy to remember. Good slogans express the characteristics of local areas in one word. Slogans can express the basic concept of various plans as a unified idea. They should not be made to end up as mere slogans.

Graphic Symbols

The badges, symbol marks, character marks, pictographs, etc., of towns are towns' graphic symbols. Town badges and symbol marks are essentially the same thing. Recently, however, many towns are adopting new and modern symbol marks which appeal to the public, while retaining old symbol marks.

Colors

Some towns have their own colors which they use as their symbols. Looking at Shimoda Town's symbol colors of "carrot red," "pastoral green," and "blue sky," we can imagine its special firm product, green fields and a blue clear sky in Aomori Prefecture.

Naming

The same as slogans, names are also a very important factor. "The path of philosophy" in Kyoto, and "unfilial streets," the name given to a street leading to a cramming school in Fukuoka City for students preparing for university entrance examinations, and a path leading to the bicycle race track in Kawasaki City—they are hit naming. "Brahms lane" at Harajuku in Tokyo has been talked about greatly. When new names are given to something, candidate names are collected from the public, in most cases. In that case, it is necessary to carry out surveys extensively and seek experts' views. Streets, parks, facilities, local products, etc., are the objects of naming.

Logotype

Logotype is used as a means to show, in letters, a town's characteristics. Its typeface is uniformly used on documents, etc., as the town's standardized style of type. If one unified logotype only is used, it will produce a refined impression. When such logotype is used, it will become possible to appeal on the image of a town.

方向案内サイン　Direction information

立花町　清刷3
平仮名ロゴタイプ

たちばな
たちばな
たちばな
たちばな
たちばな
たちばな
たちばな
たちばな
たちばな

立花町　清刷2
漢字ロゴタイプ

立花町
立花町
立花町
立花町
立花町
立花町
立花町
立花町
立花町

立花町のシンボルマーク

Tachibana city's symbol

立花町　清刷1
シンボルマーク＋ローマ字ロゴタイプ, ローマ字ロゴタイプ

TACHIBANA
TACHIBANA
TACHIBANA
TACHIBANA
TACHIBANA

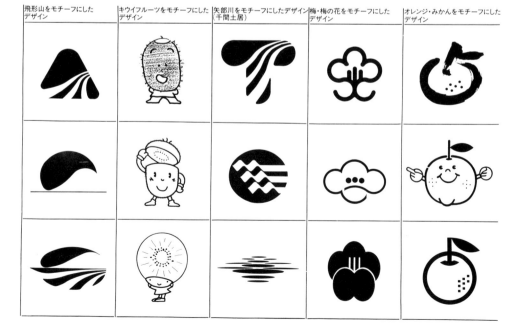

| 飛形山をモチーフにした<br>デザイン | キウイフルーツをモチーフにした<br>デザイン | 矢部川をモチーフにしたデザイン<br>（千間土居） | 梅・梅の花をモチーフにした<br>デザイン | オレンジ・みかんをモチーフにした<br>デザイン |
| --- | --- | --- | --- | --- |

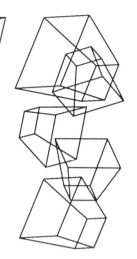

# 3.デザインの展開

Development of Designs

## 地図

まちの全体図，区画の詳細図，観光ポイント図，観光モデルルート図，交通のネットワーク図などが必要である。バラバラに表現しないで，表現を統一していけば一貫性が出てくる。

## 説明と解説

まちの沿革の説明，観光ポイントの説明，観光対象の説明，物産，宿泊，交通などの説明を統一すれば効果的である。サインのほかパンフレットやガイドブックなどにも総合的に使っていく。繰り返しの使用は住民はじめ，訪れる人へのPRともつながり，まちのイメージが内外に浸透していくに違いない。

ガイドブック，パンフレット

まちの概要紹介，観光ガイド，外国人へのインフォメーション，交通，宿泊などのガイドが必要である。同じようなパンフレットがいくつもある例が多いが，重複を避け，項目別，目的別に機能的に整理しておきたい。

## メディア

ポスター，新聞，テレビ，雑誌。公報などがある。自治体が予算を使って一般のマス・メディアを使うことはめったにないが，各種のイベントの告知や新しい施設のオープンなどはマス・メディアを使うのが効果的である。このため日頃からまちの特徴ある活動を広報活動として送りつづけ，話題の記事として取り上げられるように努力するのも必要である。まちの中に向かってはまちの公報を媒体として位置づけ，デザインにも力を入れてフルに活用することが望ましい。

## 物産

まちの物産はそれ自体がCIでありイメージ形成に役立っている。太宰府の梅が枝餅はその場でも食べられ，お土産としても評判がいい。東京・六本木の和菓子屋さんは鶯餅で有名だが，交番で場所を聞いたところ「鶯をたずねたずねて六本木」と言いながら教えてもらったことがある。掛川市の「これっしか処」では，地元の特産品を生かしたアイスクリームが大ヒットした。物産を新しく開発するのは容易ではないが，地域の特徴，産物に個性を持たせる商品開発を心掛ければ，大ヒットに結び付く道があるだろう。

この場合，商品パッケージ，ショッピングバッグ，店のPOP，ディスプレイ，解説リーフレット，店員教育などの整備が必要である。

## 事務用品

ユニフォーム，封筒，便箋，名刺，茶碗，車両なども重要なコミュニケーション・ツールである。青森県下田町の職員の名刺は，二つ折の小さな紙面を最大に利用して，地理，観光のポイント，イベント，代表的な物産が紹介されている。気負いたったところがない素朴なデザインの中に，必要なものをちゃんと伝えて，まちを知ってもらいたいという意欲が感じとれるのである。こうしたやればできるところからやる。これがまちのCIの原点である。

### Maps

It is necessary for towns to prepare various kinds of maps, starting with town maps, maps showing in detail how towns are demarcated, traffic network maps, etc. Unified designs and terms should be used in order to avoid causing an impression of disunity.

### Explanations

It will be effective if explanations are given, in a unified way, on the general outline of town, sight-seeing key points, the objects of tourism, local products, hotels, and transportation. In addition to signs, pamphlets and guidebooks should be made available. If these materials are used over and over again, they will become PR materials for town people and visitors from outside. This will certainly help the image of towns permeate inside and outside towns.

Guidebooks and pamphlets: Guidebooks and pamphlets are necessary for supplying information on the general outline of towns, tourism, transportation and hotels, especially for supplying information to foreigners. Sometimes, many pamphlets, which have similar contents to each other, are published. Overlaps and repetitions should be avoided. It will be good if they are arranged in an orderly way by item and by object.

### Media

As media, there are posters, newspapers, magazines, and gazettes. Local autonomous entities seldom appropriate budgets for the use of mass media. However, it will be effective, if they use such media when they carry out events, issue announcements, and open new facilities. In order to ensure the effective use of mass medias, it is necessary for towns to supply information on their daily activities, and have the media circles play up their activities. It is desirable to contact town people, using PR materials as media, while making full use of designs.

### Local Products

Towns' local products are in themselves CI, and they help create the image of towns. Those who visit Dazaifu can buy Umegaemochi (sweet rice cake) and eat it on the spot. The cake sells very well as a souvenir present. At Roppongi in Tokyo, there is a well-known Japanese cake shop. When I went to a police box to inquire about the location of the shop, a policeman there said jokingly, "You are looking for that shop. For that purpose only, you have come here." At "Koresshikadokoro" in Kakegawa Town, ice cream made of a special product of the town has made a big hit. It is quite a trying task to develop new products. If ingenuity is made to create new products imparting to them local characteristic, they may become hit products.

In such a case, it will become necessary to improve the package of a new product, shopping bags, POP (point of purchase) service, display, leaflets which explain a new product, the training of shop clerks etc.

### Office Supplies

A town office's uniforms, envelops, letter paper, business cards, tea pots, automobiles for use by the town are all important communications tools Personnel in the Shimoda Town office in Aomori Prefecture use the twofold small business cards on which the town's map, sightseeing key points, town events and representative products are printed. In the small space of business cards, all necessary information is stated in simple words. We can see the town's eager desire to have the town known among people. The original purpose of a town's CI is to start tackling what it can.

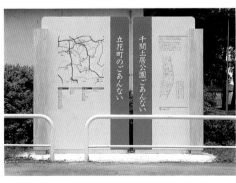

全体案内サイン　　Information sign

封筒
Envelopes

ゲートサイン
Gate sign

名刺
Business (name) cards

封筒類

Envelopes

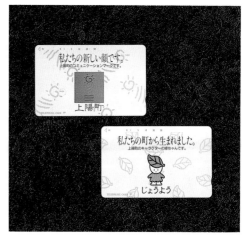

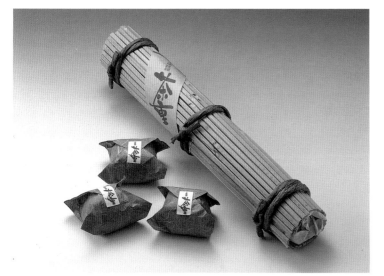

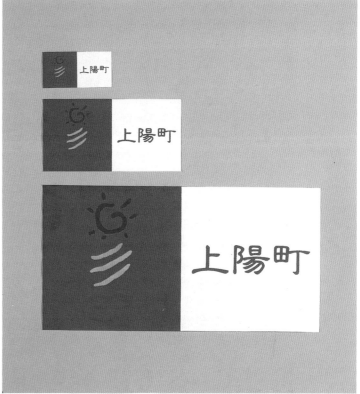

物産のパッケージ

Package of produce.

上陽町のシンボルマークとロゴタイプ

Joyo-machi's symbol and logo type.

下田町のマスコット

Shimoda's mascot.

下田町の名刺。二つ折2倍のサイズの名刺の裏表を
フルに使い，見所，下田町の位置，文化財，郷土芸
能，イベント，特産品などを的確に表現し，まちを
紹介する有効な媒体として活用している。

Shimoda's name card. By taking full advantage of
the double-size, folded card, the designer was
able to use it as an effective medium to accurately
describe the attractions, location, cultural assets,
local arts, events, and specially products of
Shimoda.

下田町の自然の美しい緑を
シンボルカラーに使いました。
爽やかで、新鮮なイメージです。

下田町の晴れ晴れとした空の青を
シンボルカラーに使いました。
力強く、意欲的なイメージです。

## 地域 CI 計画のデザインリスト

◎＝重要項目，○＝関連性のある項目

| デザイン対象 | | | 生活環境整備 | 住民活動活性化 | 愛着・誇り育成 | 観光対象開発 | 観光客対策 | 交流促進 | 産業振興・育成 | 商品・製品開発 | 販売・広報促進 |
|---|---|---|---|---|---|---|---|---|---|---|---|
| **空間** | 境界 | 町のゲート，アプローチ | ○ | | ◎ | ◎ | ◎ | ◎ | | | ○ |
| | | 交通機関 | ◎ | ○ | ◎ | ◎ | ◎ | ◎ | | | |
| | 中心 | 町の中心，象徴的な場所 | ◎ | ○ | ◎ | ○ | ○ | ◎ | | | ◎ |
| | | インフォメーション，観光案内所 | ○ | ○ | ○ | ◎ | ◎ | ○ | | | ◎ |
| | 広場 | 休憩，散歩，飲食 | ◎ | ◎ | ◎ | ○ | ○ | ◎ | | | |
| | | 市，催物 | ◎ | ◎ | ◎ | ○ | ○ | ◎ | ○ | ○ | ○ |
| | | 象徴的な彫刻，記念碑等 | ◎ | ○ | ◎ | ○ | ○ | ○ | | | |
| | 公園 | 歴史的な公園(城，庭園等) | ◎ | ○ | ◎ | ◎ | ◎ | ○ | | | |
| | | 施設型公園(遊園地等) | ◎ | ○ | ◎ | ○ | ○ | ○ | | | |
| | | 文化型公園(美術館，ホール等) | ◎ | ○ | ◎ | ○ | ○ | ○ | | | |
| | | 自然公園(森，山，海等) | ◎ | ○ | ◎ | ○ | ○ | ○ | | | |
| | 道 | 道路，階段，橋，高速道路 | ◎ | | ○ | ○ | ○ | ○ | | | |
| | | モール，遊歩道，サイクリング道路等 | ◎ | ○ | ◎ | ○ | ○ | ○ | | | |
| **表情** | 素材 | ペーブメント，建物の素材 | ◎ | | ◎ | ○ | ○ | | | | |
| | | サイン，その他の工作物の素材 | ◎ | | ○ | ○ | ○ | | | | |
| | 装飾 | 歴史的・文化的表現 | ◎ | ○ | ◎ | ◎ | ◎ | ○ | | ◎ | ◎ |
| | | 建物の外装，色彩 | ◎ | | ○ | ○ | ○ | | | | |
| | | 屋外広告物のコントロール | ◎ | | ○ | ○ | ○ | | | | ◎ |
| | 彫刻 | シンボル，ランドマーク，記念碑 | ◎ | ○ | ◎ | ○ | ○ | ○ | | ○ | ◎ |
| | | 遊具，彫刻 | ◎ | ○ | ◎ | ○ | ○ | ○ | | | ○ |
| | | 建物付帯彫刻 | ○ | ○ | ◎ | ○ | ○ | | | | ○ |
| | 植物 | 自然保護，街路樹 | ◎ | ○ | ◎ | ◎ | ○ | | | | |
| | | 植栽，内外の装飾植物，プランター | ◎ | ○ | ◎ | ○ | ○ | | | | ○ |
| | | 地域の特徴的な植物，街路の演出 | ◎ | ○ | ◎ | ○ | ○ | | | | ○ |
| | 水 | 海，湖，川，ウォーターフロント | ◎ | ○ | ◎ | ◎ | ○ | | | | |
| | | 噴水，井戸，雨の景色等 | ◎ | ○ | ◎ | ○ | ○ | | | | |
| **装置** | サイン | 都市サイン | ◎ | ◎ | ◎ | ○ | ○ | | | | ○ |
| | | 住宅地域サイン | ◎ | ◎ | ◎ | | | | | | |
| | | 公園サイン | ◎ | ○ | ◎ | ○ | ○ | | | | |
| | | 交通サイン | ◎ | ○ | ◎ | ○ | ○ | | | | ○ |
| | | 公共施設サイン | ◎ | ○ | ◎ | ○ | ○ | | | | |
| | | 広告サイン(屋外広告物) | ○ | ○ | ○ | ○ | ○ | ○ | | | |
| | | ランドマーク | ◎ | ○ | ◎ | ○ | ○ | | | | |
| | ファニチュア | 整形系ファニチュア | ◎ | ○ | ◎ | ○ | ○ | | | | |
| | | 管理系ファニチュア | ◎ | ○ | ○ | ○ | ○ | | | | |
| | | 照明系ファニチュア | ◎ | ○ | ◎ | ○ | ○ | | | | |
| | | 演出系ファニチュア | ◎ | ○ | ◎ | ○ | ○ | ○ | | | ○ |
| | | 生活系ファニチュア | ◎ | ○ | ○ | ○ | ○ | | | | |
| | | 施設系ファニチュア | ◎ | ○ | ○ | ○ | ○ | | | | |
| **活動** | 自然 | 保護，育成，活用 | ◎ | ○ | ◎ | ○ | ◎ | | | | |
| | | 整備，アピール | ◎ | ○ | ◎ | ○ | ◎ | | | | |
| | | 観光地点，自然とふれあう場の開発 | ◎ | ○ | ◎ | ○ | ◎ | | | | ○ |
| | 歴史・文化 | 記録 | ◎ | ○ | ◎ | ○ | ○ | ○ | | ○ | ○ |
| | | 保存，修復 | ◎ | ○ | ◎ | ○ | ○ | ○ | | | |
| | | クローズアップ | ◎ | ○ | ◎ | ○ | ○ | ○ | ○ | ○ | ○ |
| | | 新しい蓄積 | ◎ | ○ | ◎ | ○ | ○ | ○ | ○ | ○ | ○ |
| | 住民活動 | 生活様式 | ◎ | ◎ | ◎ | | | ○ | ○ | ○ | ○ |
| | | 住民構成 | ◎ | ◎ | ◎ | | | ○ | ○ | ○ | ○ |
| | | 教育環境 | ◎ | ◎ | ◎ | | | ○ | ◎ | | |
| | | 祭，博覧会，市，催物 | ◎ | ◎ | ◎ | ○ | ○ | ◎ | ○ | ○ | ○ |
| | 媒体 | インフォメーション | ○ | ◎ | ◎ | ◎ | ◎ | ◎ | ○ | ○ | ◎ |
| | | 広報(TV，ラジオ，新聞，雑誌) | ○ | ◎ | ◎ | ◎ | ○ | ◎ | ○ | ○ | ◎ |
| | | 商品計画，物産，土産，パッケージ | ◎ | ◎ | ◎ | ○ | ○ | ◎ | ◎ | ◎ | ◎ |
| | | 文化事業計画 | ◎ | ◎ | ◎ | ◎ | ◎ | ◎ | ○ | ○ | ◎ |

## DESIGN LIST FOR REGIONAL IDENTITY SYSTEM

◎＝IMPORTANT ITEMS, ○＝SOME CASES

| DESIGN OBJECT | | | INHABITANTS LIVING ENVIRONMENT | INHABITANTS RESIDENT CONSTITUTION | INHABITANTS AFFECTION,PRIDE,SATISFACTION | VISITORS SIGHTSEEING DEVELOPMENT | VISITORS VISITOR COUNTERMEASURE | VISITORS CULTURAL EXCHANGE | PRODUCTS INDUSTRY PROMOTE,ENCOURAGE | PRODUCTS GOODS,PRODUCTS,DEVELOPMENT | PRODUCTS MERCHANDIZING,ADVERTISING |
|---|---|---|---|---|---|---|---|---|---|---|---|
| SPACE | BOUNDARY | TOWN GATE, APPROACH | ○ | | ◎ | ◎ | ◎ | ◎ | | | ○ |
| | | TRANSPORTATION | ◎ | ○ | ◎ | ◎ | ◎ | ◎ | | | |
| | CENTER | CENTER OF CITY, PRINCIPAL PLACE | ◎ | ○ | ◎ | ○ | ○ | ◎ | | | ◎ |
| | | INFORMATION, VISITOR CENTER | ○ | ○ | ○ | ◎ | ◎ | ○ | | | ◎ |
| | OPEN SPACE | RESTING, WALKING, EAT AND DRINKING | ◎ | ◎ | ◎ | ○ | ○ | ◎ | | | |
| | | MARKET, FAIR, EVENTS | ◎ | ◎ | ◎ | ○ | ○ | ◎ | ○ | ○ | ○ |
| | | SYMBOL, MONUMENT | ◎ | ○ | ◎ | ○ | ○ | ○ | | | |
| | PARK | HISTORICAL PARK (CASTLE,GARDEN etc.) | ◎ | ○ | ◎ | ◎ | ◎ | ○ | | | |
| | | FACILITIES PARK (RECREATION GROUND etc.) | ◎ | ○ | ◎ | ○ | ○ | ○ | | | |
| | | CULTURAL PARK (MUSEUM, HALL etc.) | ◎ | ○ | ◎ | ○ | ○ | ○ | | | |
| | | NATURAL PARK (FOREST, MOUNTAIN, SEA etc.) | ◎ | ○ | ◎ | ○ | ○ | ○ | | | |
| | STREET | ROAD, STAIRWAY, BRIDGE, EXPRESSWAY | ◎ | | ○ | ○ | ○ | ○ | | | |
| | | MALL, PEDESTRIAN STREET, CYCLING ROAD etc. | ◎ | ○ | ◎ | ○ | ○ | ○ | | | |
| APPEARENCE | MATERIAL | PAVEMENT, BUILDING EXTERIOR | ◎ | | ◎ | ○ | ○ | | | | |
| | | SIGNBOARD AND ANOTHER PRODUCTS | ◎ | | ○ | ○ | ○ | | | | |
| | DECORATION | HISTORICAL AND CHARACTERISTIC ORNAMENT | ◎ | ○ | ◎ | ◎ | ◎ | ○ | | ◎ | ◎ |
| | | BUILDING'S DECORATION AND COLOR | ◎ | | ○ | ○ | ○ | | | | |
| | | SIGNBOARD'S CONTROL | ◎ | | ○ | ○ | ○ | | | | ◎ |
| | STATUE | SYMBOL, LAMDMARK, MONUMENT | ◎ | ○ | ◎ | ○ | ○ | ○ | | ○ | ◎ |
| | | PLAYTHING, STATUE | ◎ | ○ | ◎ | ○ | ○ | ○ | | | ○ |
| | | BUILDING SCULPTURE | ○ | ○ | ◎ | ○ | ○ | | | | ○ |
| | PLANTS | NATURE PROTECTION, STREET TREES | ◎ | ○ | ◎ | ◎ | ○ | | | | |
| | | PLANTS FOR EXTERIOR, INTERIOR, PLANTS BOX | ◎ | ○ | ◎ | ○ | ○ | | | | ○ |
| | | CHARACTERISTIC PLANTS, PRODUCE ON STREET | ◎ | ○ | ◎ | ○ | ○ | | | | ○ |
| | WATER | SEA, LAKE, DAM, RIVER, WATER FRONT | ◎ | ○ | ◎ | ◎ | ○ | | | | |
| | | FOUNTAIN, WELL, RAIN'S SCENE | ◎ | ○ | ◎ | ○ | ○ | | | | |
| EQUIPMENT | SIGN | TOWN SIGN | ◎ | ◎ | ◎ | ○ | ○ | | | | ○ |
| | | RESIDENTAL SECTION SIGN | ◎ | ◎ | ◎ | | | | | | |
| | | PUBLIC GARDEN (PARK) SIGN | ◎ | ○ | ◎ | ○ | ○ | | | | |
| | | TRAFFIC SIGN | ◎ | ○ | ◎ | ○ | ○ | | | | ○ |
| | | PUBLIC FACILITIES SIGN | ◎ | ○ | ◎ | ○ | ○ | | | | |
| | | ADVERTISEMENT SIGN | ○ | ○ | ○ | ○ | ○ | ○ | | | |
| | | LANDMARK | ◎ | ○ | ◎ | ○ | ○ | | | | |
| | FURNITURE | PAVEMENT ELEMENTS | ◎ | ○ | ◎ | ○ | ○ | | | | |
| | | ADMINISTER AND SAFETY ELEMENTS | ◎ | ○ | ○ | ○ | ○ | | | | |
| | | LIGHTING ELEMENTS | ◎ | ○ | ◎ | ○ | ○ | | | | |
| | | IMAGE UP ELEMENTS | ◎ | ○ | ◎ | ○ | ○ | ○ | | | ○ |
| | | LIVING (ACTIVITY) ELEMENTS | ◎ | ○ | ○ | ○ | ○ | | | | |
| | | FACILITIES ELEMENTS | ◎ | ○ | ○ | ○ | ○ | | | | |
| BEHAVIOR | NATURE | PROTECTION, CARE, USE | ◎ | ○ | ◎ | ○ | ◎ | | | | |
| | | ARRANGEMENT, APPEAL | ◎ | ○ | ◎ | ○ | ◎ | | | | |
| | | ATTRACTION POINT, DEVELOPMENT | ◎ | ○ | ◎ | ○ | ◎ | | | | ○ |
| | HISTORY, CULTURE | RECORD, MEMORIAL | ◎ | ○ | ◎ | ○ | ○ | ○ | | ○ | ○ |
| | | PRESERVATION, REPAIRING | ◎ | ○ | ◎ | ○ | ○ | ○ | | | |
| | | CLOSE UP | ◎ | ○ | ◎ | ○ | ○ | ○ | ○ | ○ | ○ |
| | | ACCUMULATION | ◎ | ○ | ◎ | ○ | ○ | ○ | ○ | ○ | ○ |
| | ACTIVITY | LIVING PATTERN | ◎ | ◎ | ◎ | | | ○ | ○ | ○ | ○ |
| | | RESIDENT CONSTITUTION | ◎ | ◎ | ◎ | | | ○ | ○ | ○ | ○ |
| | | EDUCATION ENVIRONMENT | ◎ | ◎ | ◎ | | | ○ | ◎ | | |
| | | FESTIVAL, EXHIBITION, FAIR, MARKET | ◎ | ◎ | ◎ | ○ | ○ | ◎ | ○ | ○ | ○ |
| | MEDIA | INFORMATION, PUBLICITY | ○ | ◎ | ◎ | ◎ | ◎ | ◎ | ○ | ○ | ◎ |
| | | ADVERTISING (TV, RADIO, NEWSPAPER, MAGAZINE) | ○ | ◎ | ◎ | ◎ | ○ | ◎ | ○ | ○ | ◎ |
| | | MERCHANDISING, GOODS, GIFT, PACKAGE | ◎ | ◎ | ◎ | ○ | ○ | ◎ | ◎ | ◎ | ◎ |
| | | CULTURAL PROJECT | ◎ | ◎ | ◎ | ◎ | ◎ | ◎ | ○ | ○ | ◎ |

## あとがき

　ドイツの社会心理学者、クルト・レヴィン（Kurt Lewin)は、「社会科学における場の理論」の中で学習による意識の変化を説明しているが、人々が何に価値を認めるかは学習によって変化する。現代のめまぐるしく変化する社会の中で、その時代性を微妙に反映した価値観の変化がある。

　日本が経済の高度成長を遂げた時代は、生産優先、能率主義、効率や経済性がすべてであり、人のためのまちづくりや景観づくりを重視するよりも、いかに機能的な空間をつくるかに比重がかけられていた。ところが現代はいささか状況が違ってきていて、どんなものをつくる場合でもその意義が問われ、個性や快適性や景観への配慮が要求されるようになってきた。それらは従来のモノづくりの手法ではなかなか解決できないもので、記号や情報などのコミュニケーションの観点からのコンセプトづくりが重要な意味を持ってきた。

　21世紀を目前に控えてわれわれは、世界的な位置付けの中の日本の、その中の特色あるひとつの地域であるという明確なアイデンティティを持つ、新しいまちづくりを目指している。高度情報化社会と言われ、無数の情報が交錯し、世界中の生活の様子も映像によって瞬時に伝えられる。まちづくりについての理解も昔とは大きな隔たりがある。しかし、それが技術の高度化と普及を推し進めている一方、画一化や旧来の地域文化の崩壊などの問題も深刻である。日本語の「情報」は「情けの報せ」と書く意味深いことばだが、豊富な情報から形だけではなく、人々の考え方を理解し、あくまでも現場を基本にした心のこもった人間環境をつくることが今日の課題である。

　堅苦しい論文の形式をとらず、できるだけ平易に資料の提供と提言を心掛けたのは、少数の専門家のためだけではなく、万人が望む幸せとそれを実現しようとしている多くの人々の努力を、研究者のひとりとして支援しようと願ったことと、ひとつとして同じ答えがないまちづくりの課題に直面している関係者が、地域にふさわしい答を自ら引き出して欲しかったからである。

　いささか結論を急ぐあまり、舌たらずの感を免れないが、ひとりひとりの生活やまちとのかかわりをトータルにとらえ、新しい時代へのまちづくりのヒントを提示しようとしたもので、意とするところを了解していただきたい。前の世代の人々は利便性の高い都市を実現してきたが、この功績をふまえて快適で独自の文化を誇れるまちづくりをし、次の世代に継承していきたい。コミュニケーションを中心としたデザインの考え方は、そのためにささやかな貢献をするにちがいない。こうした意味で本書が地域の開発やまちづくりに携わっている方々の発想の手がかりになることを願っている。

　本書の中の資料の提供等について定村俊満氏（株式会社ジーエー・タップ）、宮本守久氏（九州芸術工科大学）、伊原久裕氏（九州芸術工科大学）をはじめ、多くの方々のご協力をいただきました。厚くお礼申し上げます。

　なお、本書の編集に当たってグラフィック社の鶴九皋氏にアドバイスをいただき、専門分野を超える領域へのアプローチを試みることができた。エディトリアル・デザインについて気鋭の三枝英徳氏、翻訳をレスリー・ハリントンさんのご助力をいただいて出版にこぎつけることができた。その他多くの方々のご協力に心からお礼申し上げます。

6．デザイン・シミュレーション、アーネスト・バーデン、デルファイ研究所
7．シンボル・サイン国際統一化への34の提案、アメリカ・グラフィック・アーツ協会＋アメリカ運輸省　監修、宣伝会議
8．JISハンドブック・図記号、日本規格協会
9．ストリートファニチュア、西沢健、鹿島出版会
10．街のサイン計画、宮沢功、鹿島出版会
11．ピクトグラム・デザイン、太田幸夫、朗文堂
12．都市の景観、G・カレン、鹿島出版会
13．景観の構造、樋口忠彦、技報堂
14．社会科学における場の理論、クルト・レヴィン、誠信書房
15．パブリックデザイン事典、パブリックデザイン事典編集委員会編・稲次敏郎他、産業調査会

# 参考文献

1．新しい街路のデザイン、デザイン委員会＋イギリス都市計画協会、鹿島出版会
2．景観からのまちづくり、鳴海邦碩編、学芸出版会
3．The Visual Elements of Landscape, John A.Jakle, Univ. of Massachusetts Press
4．Public Streets for Public Use, Edited by Anne Vernez Moudon, VNR
5．楽しく歩ける街、OECD編、PARCO
6．デザイン・シミュレーション、アーネスト・バーデン、デルファイ研究所
7．シンボル・サイン国際統一化への34の提案、アメリカ・グラフィック・アーツ協会＋アメリカ運輸省　監修、宣伝会議
8．JISハンドブック・図記号、日本規格協会
9．ストリートファニチュア、西沢健、鹿島出版会
10．街のサイン計画、宮沢功、鹿島出版会
11．ピクトグラム・デザイン、太田幸夫、朗文堂
12．都市の景観、G・カレン、鹿島出版会
13．景観の構造、樋口忠彦、技報堂
14．社会科学における場の理論、クルト・レヴィン、誠信書房
15．パブリックデザイン事典、パブリックデザイン事典編集委員会編・稲次敏郎他、産業調査会

著者略歴　佐藤　優　（さとう　まさる）
九州芸術工科大学助教授
日本デザイン学会会員
日本サイン学会会員（理事）
日本サインデザイン協会会員（理事）他

主な業績　福岡市都市サイン（1988年SDA賞）
Problems of Visual Elements in Urban Space, IATSS Reserch Vol.3, 1978
トータル・ランドスケープ＆サイン（共著）グラフィック社
パブリックデザイン事典（共著）、産業調査会

**Masaru Sato**

Assciate Professor of Kyushu Institute of Design
**Member of**
Japan Society of Science of Design
Japan Society for Science
Japan Sign Design Association
**Works**
Fukuoka City's Sign System, 1988 SDA Prize
Problems of Visual Elements in Urban Space, IATSS Reserch Vol. 3,　1978
Urban Signage Design, Graphic-sha
Public Design Cyclopedia, Sangyo Chosa-kai

スタッフ　企画・編集　鶴　九皋
　　　　　デザイン　　三枝英徳
　　　　　　　　　　　西森千代子
　　　　　　　　　　　（株）プレゼンツ
　　　　　翻訳　　　　レスリー・ハリントン
　　　　　和文写植　　浜田　健/引間宣子
　　　　　英文写植　　大田伊三松　Lee Mei Lien

**Staff:**　Editorial Director:　Kyuko Tsuru
　　　　　Art Director:　　　Hidenori Mieda
　　　　　　　　　　　　　　Chiyoko Nishimori
　　　　　Translator:　　　　Leslie Harrington
　　　　　Typographic:　　　Ken Hamada
　　　　　Japanese Typesetter: Nobuko Hikima
　　　　　English Typesetter:　Isamatsu Ota
　　　　　　　　　　　　　　Lee Mei Lien

コミュニティデザイン　魅力あるまちづくりとイメージ計画

**COMMUNITY DESIGN**

Elements of Modern Environmental Landscape and Signage

1992年1月25日初版第1刷発行
　　　　　著者　　　　佐藤　優（さとう　まさる）
　　　　　発行者　　　久世利郎
　　　　　印刷所　　　錦明印刷株式会社
　　　　　製本　　　　大口製本株式会社
　　　　　和文写植　　三和写真工芸株式会社
　　　　　英文写植　　グローバル・メディア株式会社
　　　　　発行所　　　株式会社グラフィック社
　　　　　　　　　　　〒102　東京都千代田区九段北1-9-12
　　　　　　　　　　　電話 03-3263-4318 (代表) FAX 03-3263-5297
　　　　　　　　　　　振替・東京3-114345